THE ULTIMATE CONVERGENCE

AN END TIMES PROPHECY OF THE GREATEST SHOCK AND AWE DISPLAY EVER TO HIT PLANET EARTH

BEN R. PETERS

The Ultimate Convergence

Published by
KINGDOM SENDING CENTER
P. O. Box 25
Genoa, IL 60135

www.kingdomsendingcenter.org
ben.peters@kingdomsendingcenter.org

ISBN 13: 978-0-9789884-6-3
ISBN 10: 0-9789884-6-9

Cover and book design by *www.ChristianBookDesign.com*

Endorsements for
THE ULTIMATE CONVERGENCE

This is a book that will help launch you into the future. In it, Ben Peters gives us a fascinating look at the movement of the hand of God from the Garden of Eden until the present day. I agree that *The Ultimate Convergence* is imminent and I am excited with all that God is poised to do. You will love this book!

~ C. Peter Wagner, Apostolic Ambassador
Global Spheres, Inc.

It has been said that to know and be able to handle the future, one must study the past. In his book, *The Ultimate Convergence*, Ben Peters has done a masterful job of recounting both biblical and recent church history and combining it with the current and coming move of the Spirit. The prophetic insight and historical research in the book combines to bring the reader a tool that will empower them for the coming times of what the Lord is doing in and through the body of Christ. Read and digest this great resource and apply its revelation and you will no doubt be equipped for the next stage of your journey with the Lord.

~ David Tomberlin, David Tomberlin Ministries,
International Revivalist

Ben Peters has combined a panoramic review of God's plan of redemption with startling prophetic insight, to produce a warm and loving vision of God's work in the world today. If you are looking for a book that summarizes God's heavenly ways and His purposes with the 21st century we live in, look no further than *The Ultimate Convergence.* Once you read this book you will have a greater appreciation for how God fulfills His purposes in men and how to cooperate with Him to finish what He started. This is an exciting vision and one I know you will enjoy.

~ Joan Hunter, Joan Hunter Ministries,
International Healing Evangelist

There is a new age on the horizon. This is a time in which we will see the culmination of thousands of years of prophecy and prayers—a grand finale, a final convergence, a restoration of all things. The Tabernacle of David is being restored in the earth and a group of hungry, lovesick worshipers are arising with high praise in their mouths and a two-edged sword in their hands! In his book, *The Ultimate Convergence*, Ben Peters does an exceptional job of framing a timeline that starts in the heart of the Father, moves through creation, the prophets, early church, present day revivals, and then releases incredible prophetic insight for what is to come. If you're hungry for both revelatory teaching straight from the Word and also prophetic revelation for the days ahead, you will thoroughly enjoy The Ultimate Convergence!

- Jeff Jansen, Founder of Global Fire Ministries International,
Cofounder of Global Fire Church & World Miracle Center,
Nashville / Murfreesboro, TN,
Author of Glory Rising

Jesus' word from Matthew 13:39 – "the harvest is at the end of the age" has gained new meaning for me since reading Ben Peters' new book *The Ultimate Convergence*. I couldn't put it down! Indeed, the "Harvest" that has been prophesied is coming and it could well be called, as Ben puts it, a "convergence of dozens or even hundreds of separate entities to produce an amazing display of SHOCK AND AWE." What many "prophets" have been seeing since the 80's and 90's finds it's most clear expression in this book. It has a strong biblical foundation and I recommend this work to anyone who is waiting for the "The Great Harvest," or should I now say, "The Great Convergence"!

- Jim Paul, Senior Pastor of EastGate Christian Fellowship, Hamilton,
itinerant prophetic minister, author of Prophecy In Practice

CONTENTS

ONE

SHOCK AND AWE ~ THE COMING CONVERGENCE FINALE

Come with me please on an extremely exciting journey into the future. This book is a prophecy about what is very shortly to come, as God surprises the unsuspecting world with an incredible display of "SHOCK AND AWE!" No, there is no clear chapter and verse to prove this prophetic scenario. If there was, there would be no surprise and very little shock and awe when it did take place. However, there certainly are hints and clues to those who are reading God's Holy Word and listening to the voice of the Holy Spirit with open hearts.

Convergence has been a hot buzz-word in Kingdom streams for the past few years. I believe God is speaking now to His church, His Kingdom people, that there is much more to convergence than previously understood. In fact, I believe that God is preparing for the greatest convergence of natural and spiritual elements of all time, in preparation for His great harvest and the coming back to earth of His Beloved Son, Jesus Christ.

Whenever God chose to inhabit an earthly dwelling place, significant preparations were made for His coming. Detailed specifications were given for each chosen habitation, including the style of building, the style of worship, the financing of the structure and the way He manifested His presence. What I would like to examine is the potentially explosive phenomenon that would occur if a substantial number of these characteristics converged simultaneously on the earth.

Jesus' first coming to earth was designed, for the most part, to be a veiled, hidden event. And yet, God had prepared the convergence of many elements of history. Jesus came when the world was at peace under the Roman Empire. There were well-developed roads for transportation, and a common Greek language was extensively used. Some even believe there was a convergence of stars and/or planets that merged to form the star seen by the magi.

To get started, let's see what Webster says about the word convergence:

DEFINITION OF CONVERGENCE

1. The act of converging and especially moving toward union or uniformity; especially: coordinated movement of the two eyes so that the image of a single point is formed on corresponding retinal areas
2. The state or property of being convergent
3. Independent development of similar characters (as of bodily structure of unrelated organisms or cultural traits) often associated with similarity of habits or environment
4. The merging of distinct technologies, industries, or devices into a unified whole

Let's consolidate these points into a simple practical definition.

CONVERGENCE: The coming together in the same place at the same time of two or more entities in such a way that they become part of each other and/or of a bigger entity.

Convergence can take place with just two entities merging at the same place at the same time. The convergence of sodium and chloride can produce something totally different than either element; a substance we call "salt". A big hurricane converging with a weakened levy in New Orleans can produce an incredible disaster. An economic downturn converging with the appearance of a charismatic "knight in shining armor" can produce a major political earthquake. But the converging of continuing bad economic news with certain media continually exposing a socialist political agenda can produce a reactionary political earthquake.

In the realm of the Kingdom of Heaven on the earth, the convergence of a sickness in the family of an unbeliever with a divine appointment with someone with the gift of healing can produce a transformation of the hearts and lives of the family. The convergence of a serious financial need with a prophetic word of knowledge which is fulfilled and meets that financial need, can also turn a man's cold heart towards God.

Indeed, as we walk with God on our individual and corporate journeys, we surely experience hundreds or thousands of divine convergences that affect our lives and the lives of others around us. These convergences remind us that God is a supernatural God and He reveals Himself to us in innumerable special ways.

If just two converging entities can shake up the weather or the politics of a nation or change the spirituality of a family or a country, then what would happen if God chose to create the ultimate divine convergence of dozens or even hundreds of separate entities to produce an amazing display of "SHOCK AND AWE"?

Perhaps the best illustration of this kind of convergence is the climactic finale of a great fireworks display on the Fourth of July. For half an hour or more we see one or two beautiful displays light up the sky at a time. We see great detail and hear the sounds of individual explosions. We admire each individual event designed to delight our senses.

When it comes time to wrap things up, an incredible barrage of fireworks is unleashed with a myriad of consecutive, rapid-fire explosions of the brightest and loudest pyrotechnics available. It is a massive convergence of many different types of fireworks, which is a display designed to create a feeling of awe and amazement as it transforms the dark night into broad daylight.

But no fireworks, or any other historical phenomenon, can compare with what I believe is coming. As the great final harvest revivals begin, the world will light up, and the darkest corners of the world will be illuminated with the glorious fires. Stay with me as we look at just a few of the glorious convergences that will surely come, as the church experiences the great and glorious finale. You will find your mouth watering for the joyous and unprecedented adventure awaiting you and the world.

TWO

THE ULTIMATE INTENTION OF THE FATHER

What is God's purpose and plan for the final stage of the final age? In the book of Ephesians, Paul clearly reveals the final state of creation, when all the changes of the ages have been completed. In Ephesians 1:10, he declares the following:

> That in the dispensation of the fullness of the times He might gather in one all things in Christ, both which are in heaven and which are on earth – in Him.

Paul is describing nothing less than an enormous convergence of everything in existence. Everything (with the exception of the devil, his slaves and the lake of fire) will be seen as part of Jesus; His glorious majesty will encompass His bride and His creation. All will be clothed in the righteousness of Christ and will become a very real part of Him. Because we have natural minds, our understanding is obviously limited in this dimension of reality. Paul is speaking of spiritual realities that can be known only in the dimension of the spirit.

The key thought here though is that God loves unity – oneness – and He has gone to great lengths to illustrate that. In "God's Favorite Number," I detailed a number of times and places where God said, "Two shall become one." It wasn't just man and wife, but also Israel and Judah (Ezekiel 37: 15-28), Jews and Gentiles, male and female, Jesus and His Father, Jesus and His disciples, etc.

But what about the coming visitation? Will there really be a coming together of many powerful and positive influences at the same time?

Will there someday be real unity in the body of Christ?

Will there be a generation with a great and passionate desire to serve the King?

Will there be a huge transfer of wealth from the godless to the godly, in order to equip and send that generation into the harvest fields of the earth?

Will there be a huge renaissance of Christian art, drama, music, literature, movies, technology, etc.?

Will there be Christians who discover new technologies and develop inventions that help solve major problems on planet earth?

Will there be Christians developing new medicines and discovering health secrets that will give people a much longer life and a greater quality of life at the same time?

Most importantly, will there be a restoration of the glory and power of the early church with signs, wonders and miracles producing wave after wave of souls coming into the Kingdom?

Will the church multiply and find favor with God and man?

Will people be transported like Philip?

Will there be an increase in major creative miracles and the raising of the dead?

Will there be a resurgence of angelic activity?

Will people have greater and more frequent visions, dreams and Heavenly visitations?

Will there be revivals of repentance like in the Great Awakenings?

Will there also be revival phenomena like the outbreak of laughter, shaking, falling and apparent drunkenness?

Will there be signs and wonders like gold dust, feathers falling from the ceiling, etc.?

Will people, like Joseph and Daniel, be anointed to rise up and take political leadership positions in the world?

Will they be able to reduce injustice and human rights abuses in society and in the darker places of the world?

Will the hearts of the fathers turn to the children and the hearts of the children to the fathers?

Will the generations work together to accomplish incredible change on the earth?

Will there be intimacy with God and worship that never ends like it was in David's tabernacle?

Will there be the wisdom and wealth of Solomon's reign?

Will there be a whole new level of understanding of the written Word of God, and a greater ability to interpret the prophetic books of Daniel and Revelation?

Will there be clear prophetic words about events in the immediate future?

I have surely missed a wide variety of blessings coming to the earth, as the way is prepared for the Second Coming of Christ. The list above will give you an idea of what could happen.

Let's check out some of the possibilities from our common history and get excited about the potential of the ULTIMATE CONVERGENCE happening in our lifetimes. You may have many skeptical thoughts in response to these ideas, based on your previous understanding of prophecy, but stay with me. Those thoughts will be addressed and hopefully your concerns will be dispelled.

THREE

THE GARDEN OF EDEN

Throughout biblical history, God has repeatedly expressed His desire or passion to place Himself in the middle of the people that He created for Himself. Examples of this are seen in the Garden of Eden, in the wilderness wanderings with Moses' Tabernacle, in David's Tabernacle, in Jesus' first coming, in the early church and finally in the book of Revelation. There are actually many more examples, and we will look at a number of them in the following pages.

A QUICK LOOK AT CREATION

Before going to the Garden of Eden, we should first go back to the time of creation itself. In the beginning, God had to prepare the earth because it was formless and void. He sent His Holy Spirit to brood or hover over the waters that covered the earth. Today, we could say that the earth is spiritually formless and void. What God did then is what He is doing now. Just as a mother hen hovers over her eggs until the chicks make their entrance into the world of light, so is the Holy Spirit hovering over the earth today.

Once again, in these days before the great harvest of souls, the Holy Spirit is brooding over churches, prayer groups, cities and regions of the earth, bringing them to maturity until they are ready to be released into an unsuspecting society.

When we lived on the coast of Washington, we had a few chickens. They would occasionally escape their pen and roam the yard and surrounding woods. Unknown to us, one of the hens had escaped and laid many eggs. One day, much to our surprise, we heard the cheeping of baby chicks in the woods. We discovered our missing hen, and she had a dozen or so chicks following her around. We were only able to corral them when we recorded the clucking of the mother hen and played it loudly at the edge of the woods where the chicks were hiding. They walked right up to the tape recorder, believing their mother to be there.

Even so, the incubation of the harvesters is taking place out of sight and under the radar of the leaders of this world. The time will surely come when, in divine coordination with many other converging events and entities, they will emerge from under the covering wings of the Holy Spirit. They will dispense light and the glory of God into every dark place, making their mark on the world.

GOD"S GARDEN

As always, when God was planning a visitation, He prepared a place where He could meet with man. In the book of Genesis, God prepared the Garden of Eden, a place of pleasure and beauty, where man and woman would enjoy their surroundings and where He could enjoy their company.

We read in Genesis 2:9 that God made every tree that was pleasant to the eyes and good for food. God never just provided for man's minimum needs; He always showed His loving and artistic side as well. He created the garden and the trees to appeal to man's senses and provide special enjoyment for him. We can only speculate as to the colors and fragrances that delighted the senses in this special place, but we can be very certain that it surpassed the most beautiful gardens on the earth today.

After the temptation and sin of Adam and Eve, God came walking in the garden, which was probably a common occurrence. While most translations say that He came "in the cool of the day", the word "cool" is actually the Hebrew word "ruach", which means "wind, breath or spirit". The word "cool" implies that there was a "hot" part of the day, which would be unpleasant and incompatible with the concept of a place like paradise. Because of this, I tend to believe it refers to a pleasant breeze that happened, perhaps during the warmer part of the day, keeping everyone comfortably cool.

Another possibility is that the "ruach" represented the breath and the stirring of the Holy Spirit among them, as in Genesis 1:3, when the Spirit of God hovered over the face of the waters. When God said, "Let us make man in Our own image," it was obviously the Father, Son and Holy Spirit involved in creating man. If God created man for fellowship, then surely the Trinity would meet with Adam and Eve in the Garden, which God had prepared for their fellowship.

The Garden had a river flowing through it, which came out of Eden and then divided up into four rivers. People have always liked to live close to water. Rivers provide drinking water, fish to eat, water for agriculture and a means of transportation. Today, people pay extra for real estate with a view of water – whether the ocean, a lake or a river. God prepared a piece of prime real estate for Adam and Eve where they could enjoy the view together.

The first river was named Pishon, and the region where it flowed featured high quality gold. Before the fall, is it possible that the gold of this place was like the gold in Heaven – translucent like glass?

Not only was there good quality gold, but there were bdellium and onyx stones in that region also. God created this garden region with extravagance. These precious stones were ornaments strategically placed there for the pleasure of the eyes. But again, it wasn't just for Adam and Eve; it was also for God to enjoy with them. We want to make this extremely clear. God prepared a place for Himself that He could enjoy with those He had created for His own pleasure and fellowship.

We will see this truth much more clearly in the chapters ahead. I can assure you that you will be as amazed as I am with the incredibly detailed creativity that God used to prepare a place where He might dwell.

But before we get ahead of ourselves in this adventure, we need to pause and reflect upon the effect that sin had on this wonderful fellowship that God had with man and woman. How privileged Adam and Eve were to be able walk through the Garden of Eden, sharing and enjoying the exhilarating beauty of this artistic creation together!

Sadly, when sin came, so came death! It was death to intimacy with God, death to the enjoyment of the Garden of Eden, death to weed-free gardening and even eventual physical death for Adam and Eve.

However, God would not allow His purpose for creation to be thwarted. Since He knew what would happen before the creation of the world, He had a plan to restore that relationship. That plan would involve the death of His own Son, a long history of covenants with individuals and a nation that He chose to set apart from all others.

FOUR

ENOCH, NOAH, ABRAHAM

After the Edenic paradise was lost to man, God began to draw individuals to Himself for fellowship and intimacy. We see that Abel and Cain offered sacrifices to God. However, Cain's sacrifice was rejected, possibly for not involving a blood sacrifice and thus not fulfilling the symbolic prophetic picture of Jesus, the Lamb of God.

The story of Enoch is one of the greatest early story of God's dwelling with man. We know his ancestry and we know that he lived 365 years on the earth. We also know that he walked with God, but we know little else, except that God took him from the earth.

What we can obviously speculate is that God missed the intimacy that He had with Adam and Eve in the Garden of Eden. When He found a man who responded to His wooing, He revealed Himself to him in a very unique and profound way. Since there was no longer a Garden of Eden to enjoy on the earth, God found it easier to just take Enoch to Heaven, where their fellowship would be perfect.

The question could certainly be asked at this point: "Did Enoch go straight into the presence of God, or did he, like all the other Old Testament Saints, go to the holding place that Jesus referred to in the story of the rich man and Lazarus?" This question is one that I can't answer, but one I look forward to asking in the next life.

Noah was the next man who "walked with God." God observed the rampant corruption and increasing violence in the earth that He had created as a place for fellowship with Him. He determined to cleanse the earth of His own creation, but one man was different, and "Noah found grace in the eyes of the Lord." (Genesis 6:8)

God clearly told Noah that He would establish His covenant with him and replenish humanity through his little family. He shared his heart with Noah and gave him detailed plans for the ark. This ark would be a place of safety from God's wrath. It was also a type of the Ark of the Covenant, in that it enabled a new covenant with man, which was to be given to Noah and his descendants. The Ark of the Covenant was the place where God placed His strongest presence. Surely, God's presence was also on Noah's ark.

For about one hundred years, Noah and his sons built the ark, and they probably experienced frequent and special encounters with God. Since they had lived on the ark for about six months, it seems probable that God had communicated with Noah from time to time. We do know for sure that God told Noah when he was to go into the ark and when it was time to leave the ark.

When Abram came on the scene, God saw another man with whom he could develop an intimate relationship. He called Abram and made a covenant promise to him regarding his future generations. He promised to make him a great nation and that everyone who blessed him would be blessed and everyone who cursed him would be cursed.

As we discover in our study of Abraham (the new name God gave him), God became a close personal friend. In Isaiah 41:8, God calls Abraham, "My friend!" There are more than fifty references in Genesis where God and Abraham speak to each other and Abraham builds altars to God to worship Him. James 2:23 sums it up; "Abraham believed

God, and it was accounted to him for righteousness. And he was called the friend of God."

A very important truth revealed in that verse is that friendship and faith go hand in hand. Faith flows from friendship and friendship grows as friends show faith in each other. Many people want the power of faith to deliver them from their problems and circumstances. But few are willing to pay the price for friendship with God by seeking God's presence and laying down their lives for Him. A true friend does lay down his life for his friend.

Of most importance to this study is the fact that God had found a man with whom He could have intimate fellowship again, and He had found a man whose children would become a holy nation unto Him. They would be a people who would build a place for Him in their midst where He could dwell and radiate His goodness to them. They would be a people who could be a testimony to the world that He was a God that loved people and wanted to know them in a pure and intimate manner.

"For God so loved the world." (John 3:16) Yes, God was looking for a man and a nation that would demonstrate His love to the whole world. Most of Israel never figured that out; they simply thought that God liked them the best. The rest of the world was considered their enemy and an enemy of God. Sadly, even the prophet Jonah had the wrong attitude regarding the other nations. Although David, a man after God's own heart, had a passion that all the nations and people of the world would worship God, and this is clearly illustrated in many of his psalms. However, let's not get too far ahead of ourselves. Let's go back now to Abraham. Abraham's grandson, Jacob, would also have a special encounter with God and would receive a new covenant to add to what Abraham had already received.

Just one more thing before we leave Abraham. Relationship with God almost always seemed to involve giving and receiving of material or financial benefits. In the Garden of Eden, God gave it all to Adam, including the gems and the gold. Adam served God as a "zoologist", but His main service was friendship. We don't know enough about

Enoch to comment on his relationship with finances, but we know that Noah was asked to offer sacrifices to God when he left the ark.

So what about Abraham? This great patriarch is known as the first one to give tithes. After rescuing Lot and his friends from foreign invaders, Abraham gave the tithe to Melchizedek, who was the king of Salem and priest of the Most High God. Who taught Abraham the principal of tithing? It was probably not his pagan father. Most likely, he learned the principal of tithing directly from conversations with God.

FIVE

JACOB

Abraham's grandson, Jacob, was a man of a mixed reputation. He was called a deceiver, and he used his brother's weaknesses and his mother's deceitful plans to "steal" the birthright and the blessing from Esau. But one thing Jacob did have going for him was passion and determination. Not only did he get the pretty girl he wanted after twenty-one years of labor, but he had three very incredible encounters with God.

JACOB ENCOUNTERS GOD

The first encounter occurred at the place Jacob named Bethel. One night, on his journey to find his relatives and escape the wrath of Esau, Jacob laid his head on a stone and fell asleep. He dreamed a powerful dream in which a ladder was placed on the earth that reached to Heaven. Angels were ascending and descending on the ladder and God,

Himself, appeared at the top of the ladder and spoke to Jacob.

God told Jacob that He would bless him and prosper him and return him to the land of his father, Isaac, and his grandfather, Abraham. Jacob woke up from the dream and realized that he had just experienced a special visitation from God. He obviously had some revelation from God about it because he made a very insightful observation. He said, "Surely the Lord is in this place, and I did not know it." Then he added, "How awesome is this place! This is none other than the house of God, and this is the gate of heaven." (Genesis 28:16-17)

This dream can mean a lot of things to a lot of people, but this is what it means to me, as I relate it to the subject at hand. God was in His place in Heaven, while man was on his weary pilgrimage on the sin-damaged earth. However, God's desire was interaction and communication with man. Angels were being dispatched to reveal God's desires to man, but man was asleep and not really understanding God's communication. Even though God was speaking to him from the top of the ladder, Jacob discerned that God was visiting Him in a special way, and he perceived that the place he had camped for the night was actually a dwelling place for God. Jacob named the place, Bethel, which means "house of God."

THE HOUSE OF GOD AND FINANCE

Jacob responded to God's covenant promise with a covenant promise of his own. He told God that if He would be with him, protect him and prosper him, that he would give God a tithe of everything he was given. In this situation, Jacob was not donating resources to build a specific tabernacle or temple, but it was a grateful response to the fact that God had built a house of worship in the middle of the wilderness to meet with him.

A SECOND (LESS FAMOUS) ENCOUNTER

Jacob's second major encounter with God was on his way back to the land of promise, after acquiring two wives, many sons and daughters and great flocks and herds while serving his father-in-law, Laban. This is an encounter that is easily missed because it only takes up two verses in Scripture. Let's take a quick look at it.

> So Jacob went on his way, and the angels of God met him. When Jacob saw them, he said, "This is God's camp." And he called the name of that place Mahanaim. (Genesis 32:1-2)

The name, Mahanaim, actually means double camp. Perhaps Jacob was saying this is the second time I've camped with the angels of God. At any rate, he had a meeting with angels and surely this was a powerful preparation for his return to the Land of Promise, the place where God would eventually place His tabernacle and temple.

What Jacob recognized, for the second time, was that God wanted to dwell and camp among His people. We will soon see how important that concept was in God's relationship and dealings with man, the crowning achievement of God's creativity.

The third encounter with God is much better known and receives a lot more print in Scripture. After his meeting with the angels, Jacob dispatches his family and messengers to his brother Esau with gifts from his herds and flocks. Then he prays a passionate prayer to God, reminding God of His previous promise to him at Bethel – the House of God.

JACOB'S THIRD MAJOR ENCOUNTER WITH GOD

When everyone had gone, Jacob was all alone except for a "Man" who wrestled with him until the breaking of day. Jacob was allowed to win that unusual wrestling match and made his persistent petition for another heavenly blessing. The "Man" changed his name to "Israel", which means "Prince with God." This time Jacob called the name of the place Peniel, which means the "Face of God". Jacob declared, "I have seen God face to face and my life is preserved." (Genesis 32:30)

Jacob's three encounters reveal the prophetic progress of Jacob's relationship with God. Note the progression. Jacob's first encounter was with God talking to him from the top of the ladder and angels coming and going on the ladder. He recognized the place as a dwelling place for God and promised to give God tithes of all his possessions.

The second encounter was an actual meeting with angels. Although we have few details about what was discussed, Jacob again recognized a place where God had camped, and hc was in close fellowship with God's messengers. In the first encounter, Jacob saw both God and the angels at a distance. In this encounter, he met the angels like you meet people on the earth.

In the third encounter, Jacob declares that he didn't just view God from a distance, and he didn't just meet and talk to His angels. He actually saw God face to face and interacted with Him. He pressed and persisted until He got the blessing he needed from God.

Many preachers may see this as an example of how to get what we need from God, but I see something else here. I believe that God was the initiator of this process and that He desired not just to bless Jacob, but He was revealing the longing of His heart to meet with man face to face and have that intimate place in their hearts. He was yearning for that original Garden of Eden relationship. He also wanted another friend like Enoch and like Abraham.

God began His relationship with Jacob when He spoke from the top of the ladder in Jacob's dream. Then He sent His angels to meet with Jacob face to face. Finally, He appeared in human form and spent the night in a very unique form of fellowship with Jacob where Jacob could say that he had seen God face to face.

CHAPTER 6

MOSES

The life and ministry of Moses gives us an enormous amount of prophetic information about the way God prepares a place for Himself when He intends to dwell among His people. There is so much typology and foreshadowing of what was to come that this entire book could be devoted to just discussing this one subject. However, because we have so much more ground to cover, we will only be focusing on a few highlights regarding Moses, his tabernacle and the most important aspects of the subject.

Obviously, God was first preparing a man for the job. His task would be not only to lead the Children of Israel out of Egypt to the Promised Land, but most importantly, he would be called upon to build a significant dwelling place for the Presence of God. This dwelling place would, of course, be right in the very center of the camp.

Moses was chosen to be spared when other Hebrew children were being murdered. His adopted mother was none other than the daughter of the Pharaoh. As a result, he was raised in the courts of the king and developed a royalty mentality. However, Moses still identified with his own people, and he made an unwise attempt to help them by killing an Egyptian who was hurting an Israelite.

The next phase of Moses' life was living as a fugitive from his adopted grandfather. He became a shepherd, working for his wife's father. For forty years he stayed away from Egypt, seemingly without purpose or vision for his destiny. The most important lesson that Moses learned during this season was that in his own strength he could not accomplish his purpose and destiny. His self-confidence was gone and he would need to see several signs and wonders before he could believe that God could even use him at all.

Like Moses, many times our self-confidence gets us into trouble. When we become fully aware of our own insufficiency, we tend to draw near to God and appeal to Him for His help. This is where we usually develop the deepest intimacy with God and fulfill His longing for relationship with us. By the time that God appeared to Moses in the burning bush, he had lost his earlier passion for his destiny. God restored that passion and fanned the flame of his desire and dream until he was ready for one of the most amazing challenges ever faced by mortal man.

When God spoke to Moses from the burning bush, he commanded him to remove his shoes. Symbolically, God was saying that his old journey was finished. Those shoes represented his journey as "a failure," as far as his destiny was concerned. They were shepherd's shoes and he was finished working with four-footed animals. He was now ready for the greater challenge, working with two-legged sheep that were often more stubborn than the four-legged versions. Removing shoes is also symbolic of cleansing from the contamination that has been picked up in our travels. God's Presence is always Holy Ground – a place set apart for a special purpose.

After God prepared Moses to be a dwelling place for His Presence, He taught Moses how to build a dwelling place for Him to meet with the Children of Israel. Exodus 25:8 is a very significant and revealing verse. It shows God's true purpose and passion:

> And let them make Me a sanctuary, that I may dwell among them.

Notice that God didn't instruct Moses to make a tabernacle, so that the people could get their sins forgiven by making animal sacrifices. God was instead expressing His primary purpose for the sanctuary – He wanted to be close to His people whom He had created for intimate fellowship. All the detailed instructions that God gave to Moses regarding the tabernacle had to do with making a way for the people to be able to come close to Him, but it was just as much for His sake as theirs.

GOD'S PASSION FOR UNITY

Many years ago, God began to impress upon me how important unity was to Him. We know how important it was to Jesus, and we are reminded of that every time His prayer in John 17 is read. Of course, it was also important to Paul, who scolded the Corinthians more than once for their lack of unity. He also implored the church in many of his epistles, such as Ephesians and Philippians, to guard the unity that the Holy Spirit had brought to them.

Back in Exodus 26, we are given a preview of God's heart for unity:

> And you shall make fifty clasps of gold, and couple the curtains together with the clasps, so that it may be one tabernacle. (Exodus 26:6)

> And you shall make fifty bronze clasps, put the clasps in the loops, and couple the tent together, that it may be one. (Exodus 26:11)

Compare now:

> That they all may be one, as You, Father, are in Me, and I in You; that they also may be one in Us, that the world may believe that You sent Me. (John 17:21)

The tabernacle of Moses, like Solomon's temple, was a type and shadow of the body of Christ. The curtains of the tabernacle were all to be joined together. God didn't want divisions – He wanted it to be one tabernacle, just like He wanted His church – His body – to be one.

FINANCING THE TABERNACLE

When God prepared the Garden of Eden, He provided all the resources from His own infinite supply. When God encountered Jacob at Bethel, Jacob promised to tithe all of his future income if God would protect and bless him. But when it came time to build the Tabernacle, there was a brand new way of financing the sanctuary of God's presence.

It all started when the Children of Israel were preparing to depart from Egypt. Moses instructed the people, at God's command, to ask their neighbors for articles of gold and silver and clothing for the journey. God moved miraculously on their Egyptian neighbors and gave them great favor. As a result, Israel left Egypt quite wealthy in earthly treasures, a fitting stroke of justice after they had labored as slaves for many years.

When the time came to build the tabernacle and all its fancy furniture, a lot of material resources were needed. God had provided it all and had distributed it among the people, who had obediently asked their Egyptian neighbors for provisions. God now gave them the opportunity to give to Him what He had put in their hands through the Egyptians.

Let's take a look at God's offering invitation in Exodus 25. Notice the emphasis on the willing heart. No one had to give any of their treasures to God for His sanctuary. He has always loved a cheerful giver!

> Speak to the children of Israel, that they bring Me an offering. From everyone who gives it willingly with his heart you shall take My offering. And this is the offering which you shall take from them: gold, silver, and bronze; blue, purple, and scarlet

> thread, fine linen, and goats' hair, ram skins dyed red, badger skins, and acacia wood; oil for the light, and spices for the anointing oil and for the sweet incense; onyx stones, and stones to be set in the ephod and in the breastplate. (Exodus 25:2-7)

Clearly, God was teaching His people the joy of giving. As slaves in Egypt, they had little to give. Now that they had some wealth, God was teaching them how to put their priorities in order. He knew that those who gave willingly would find great fulfillment and joy in the process, especially when their giving was for a project that was so precious to the God who had so abundantly prospered and delivered them from centuries of bondage on the same night.

GOD EMPOWERS CREATIVITY FOR GLORY AND FOR BEAUTY IN HIS ARTISANS

One of the most fascinating and exciting elements of the tabernacle of Moses was the realization that God could impart a Holy Spirit anointing on men and women to create beautiful and artistic things that bring pleasure to the natural senses. The word artistic is used first in Exodus 26:1, where God gave instructions to make ten curtains "of fine woven linen and blue, purple, and scarlet thread; with artistic designs of cherubim" woven into the fabric.

The next significant reference comes in Exodus 28:

> And you shall make holy garments for Aaron, your brother, for glory and for beauty. So you shall speak to all who are gifted artisans, whom I have filled with the spirit of wisdom, that they may make Aaron's garments, to consecrate him, that he may minister to Me as priest. (Exodus 28:2-3)

Personally, I've never been into clothes. Religiously, I often reminded myself and others that God looks on the heart, not the outward appearance. Growing up on the "poor side of the tracks," I resented the rich, whom I considered proud and selfish, while I saw myself as poor and humble. It was the rich that could waste their money on expensive clothes and spend so much time talking about styles and brand names, etc.

I was also raised to be extremely practical and not as concerned with how things looked. If something was just there to look nice, it had no value to me. I liked things that could do something, not just look pretty. Of course, this has been a challenge for my wife, who is a lover of beauty. She is very careful to dress tastefully for those who see her, and she has taught me everything I know about dressing for different occasions.

The point I'm trying to make is that God is not like I was. He loves beauty and creativity. Anyone who studies His creation is amazed at the incredible variety of plants and animals, both on land and in the seas. God is incredibly creative and made things amazingly beautiful, just for our pleasure and His. Thankfully, I now have a much greater appreciation of art and beauty, and I love creativity in many realms, including writing and music.

Notice now some powerful details in the Scripture quoted above. Moses was told to speak to all who were "gifted artisans". This may be the first clear biblical reference to any spiritual gifts, as well as to the term "artisans". Then God says that He, Himself, has filled them with the "spirit of wisdom", which is one of the spiritual gifts listed in I Corinthians 12:8-10.

It wasn't until God was ready to manifest His presence in an earthly tabernacle that He gave the first revelation of the gifts of the Holy Spirit. Whenever God visits the earth in a special way, His gifts, and other spiritual activities, experience a power surge. In the above scripture, this particular gift of wisdom was released for the purpose of creating clothing for glory and beauty. In this case, the meaning of the word "glory" would be "honor" or "exaltation". God was revealing how important it was to prepare for His coming by increasing the creative and artistic abilities needed to beautify His sanctuary.

The rest of the chapter (42 verses in all) is all about the clothing and ornaments created for Aaron and his sons. This includes a breastplate, an ephod, a robe, a skillfully woven tunic, a turban and a sash (v. 4).

The garments and breastplate included threads of gold, purple, blue and scarlet. It had gold chains and onyx stones on which were inscribed the names of the twelve children of Israel. Obviously, these garments were very important to God, in that they symbolized the purity and beauty that He would put on His children who would all someday become "kings and priests" unto Him. Verse 40 reads as follows:

> For Aaron's sons you shall make tunics, and you shall make sashes for them. And you shall make hats for them, for glory and beauty.

This speaks of the unity of the older and younger generations and the passing of the spiritual inheritance from the older to the younger. It prophesies that the younger generation will also be clothed in the beauty of the Lord, radiating His glory to all who behold them.

Exodus 31 reinforces this whole concept of God's love of creativity and beauty, with a little more detail:

> See, I have called by name Bezalel, the son of Uri, the son of Hur, of the tribe of Judah. And I have filled him with the Spirit of God, in wisdom, in understanding, in knowledge, and in all manner of workmanship, to design artistic works, to work in gold, in silver, in bronze, in cutting jewels for setting in carving wood, and to work in all manner of workmanship. And I, indeed I, have appointed with him Aholiab, the son of Ahisamach, of the tribe of Dan; and I have put wisdom in the hearts of all the gifted artisans, that they may make all that I have commanded you. (Exodus 31:2-6)

Here we have the first example of two named individuals and a whole class of people that God empowered with spiritual gifts for a particular task. Once again, we see how much God cares about the way that we prepare for the coming of His presence, as well as how much He loves creativity and beauty.

It is also amazing how often God repeats the above information to Moses, each time with a little more detail. In Chapters 35 and 36, we have a repetition of chapter 31 with the added detail that God had put in the hearts of both Bezalel and Aholiab the ability to teach others what they had been gifted by God to do. Here we see the gift of wisdom being released, and then we see the teaching gift being place in the hearts of these two men.

MORE ABOUT FINANCING THE SANCTUARY

Exodus 36 gives us a wonderful nugget regarding giving. Whenever the people of God realize that God is about to manifest His presence in a new and magnificent way, there is great excitement about His coming. When that excitement occurs, almost everyone has a desire to participate and accelerate the progress to bring His presence, as we shall see again in the early church in the book of Acts.

Please read and enjoy the following six verses:

> Then Moses called Bezalel and Aholiab, and every gifted artisan in whose heart the Lord had put wisdom, everyone whose heart was stirred to come and do the work. And they received from Moses all the offering which the children of Israel had brought for the work of the service of making the sanctuary. So they continued bringing to him freewill offerings every morning."
>
> Then all the craftsmen who were doing all the work of the sanctuary came, each from the work he was doing, and they spoke to Moses, saying, "The people bring much more than enough for the service of the work which the Lord commanded us to do." So Moses gave a commandment, and they caused it to be proclaimed throughout the camp, saying, "Let neither man nor woman do any more work for the offering of the sanctuary." And the people were restrained from bringing, for the material they had was sufficient for all the work to be done – indeed too much. (Exodus 36:2-7)

What a wonderful testimony of the joyful sacrifice demonstrated when the people get excited about participating in such a wonderful event. This is a prophetic picture of the coming convergence, when God's people realize how glorious and incredible the coming of God's presence will be.

Again, keep in mind that the people were offering back to God the treasures that He had put into their hands, and they had the choice of keeping those treasures for themselves. However, the people were so excited about the coming of the presence of God to the camp in a new and special way that they gave with an excited and truly joyful heart. But because the artisans had received too many gifts, and it was taking too much of their time, they asked Moses to tell the people to stop coming.

Will this ever happen in the future? I believe it will and to an even greater degree. God has saved the best for the last. We will see His glorious and ultimate finale, which will astound the whole world and shake the gates of hell to the core.

Now let's look at what happened when the beautiful and glorious tabernacle was assembled and completed:

> Then the cloud covered the tabernacle of meeting, and the glory of the Lord filled the tabernacle. And Moses was not able to enter the tabernacle of meeting, because the cloud rested above it, and the glory of the Lord filled the tabernacle. (Exodus 40:34-35)

When the cloud of God's glory descended on the tabernacle, the presence of God was thick and heavy. Even Moses, who had been on the mountain with the Lord, was unable enter the tabernacle. When a powerful manifestation of God's presence appears on the earth, there is always a sense of the "fear of the Lord", which causes even His closest friends to fall on their faces in reverent awe.

Moses' tabernacle is indeed a powerful picture of many things which are now and yet still to come. The ultimate convergence will include the artistic beauty and glory on a generation of artisans, as well as the fear and awe of God. It will also include the excited participation in giving and receiving in material and financial ways. Additionally, it will involve many men and women who, like Moses, have had amazing encounters with God, and they will be prepared and equipped to lead His people out of bondage. A glorious and unprecedented unity will be seen in the people of God, which will supersede even the unity of the early church in many ways.

As we move on, we will see that God has other things to teach us from later manifestations of His presence. Come with me as we take a brief look at the Tabernacle of David.

SEVEN

DAVID

In many ways, David was prepared by God in a similar manner to Moses. Just as Moses was rejected by his brethren, so was David. Both were taking care of sheep when God promoted them to a higher place. Moses killed an Egyptian to save his brethren from harm. David killed a lion and a bear to save his sheep, and he killed Goliath to save Israel from their enemy.

Both Moses and David had a passion for worship and God's glory. Moses may not have played the harp or invented instruments for worship, but he was the one who begged God to show him His glory on the mountain. David, on the other hand, was a song-writer and instrument-maker, who was also called a "man after God's own heart".

Let's now examine the elements of David's tabernacle and discover what made it different from Moses' tabernacle.

WORSHIP

Although we have a couple of instances of songs written to celebrate victories, etc. during the Mosaic period, the tabernacle of Moses was known for its ceremony, not its music. It reflected the glory, beauty and majesty of God's presence, but it was quite devoid of the intimate worship that David introduced centuries later.

The tabernacle of David was so much different. Although there are fewer details given about this dwelling place for God, we do know that there was continuous worship with thousands of musicians and singers involved in a never-ending praise offering to God. According to I Chronicles 23:5, there were four thousand, who "praised the Lord with musical instruments."

One of the elements of the coming convergence is continuous worship. It has already begun in numerous cities around the world, and it is what the Father is looking for. Continuous worship entices Him to come and inhabit His people in a demonstrable way.

David was not only a musician, but he was also an inventor of musical instruments. Even much later in Hezekiah's time, it was reported that they played instruments that David had made. (II Chronicles 29:27)

There is an interesting account of how David brought the ark to his tabernacle. Even on his failed first attempt, when the ark was brought on a cart and Uzzah was struck dead when he tried to steady the ark, there was a powerful expression of the kind of tabernacle David established for the Lord. Read the following clip from II Samuel 6.

> Then David and all the house of Israel played music before the Lord on all kinds of instruments of fir wood, on harps, on stringed instruments, on tambourines, on sistrums*, and on cymbals. (II Samuel 6:5)

David, himself, was playing an instrument, and we are told that all the house of Israel played music before the Lord, which is obviously a generalization. However, it is clear that Israel had become a very musically skilled nation of worshippers.

* Sistrums were also translated as cornets in other versions. They were instruments that made a rattling sound.

When David made his second (and successful) attempt to bring the ark to the tabernacle that he had prepared, he once again interwove exuberant worship in the process. This time we are told they brought the ark with shouting, the sound of the trumpet and enthusiastic dancing by King David. He was willing to be totally undignified before the people in the presence of God, which got him into trouble with Michal, his wife, which in turn resulted in her being barren for the rest of her life.

As we know from reading the Psalms, David was first a worshipper, which, I believe, made him a "man after God's own heart". His tabernacle was not the formal ceremonial tabernacle that Moses had erected at God's command. David's tabernacle was the expression of a new level of intimacy, which brought the people closer to God through worship.

OPEN ACCESS TO THE PRESENCE OF GOD

David's tabernacle apparently had no veils separating the ark from the people. Everyone could approach the presence of God. This was prophetic of the New Testament relationship of God with man. It was in the atmosphere of worship that man was able to approach God without being struck dead.

Note the following excerpts from I Chronicles 16:

> So they brought the ark of God, and set it in the midst of the tabernacle that David had erected for it. Then they offered burnt offerings and peace offerings before God. (I Chronicles 16:1)

> And he appointed some of the Levites to minister before the ark of the Lord, to commemorate, to thank, and to praise the Lord God of Israel.
>
> Asaph the chief, and next to him Zechariah, then Jeiel, ... with stringed instruments and harps, but Asaph made music

> with cymbals; Benaiah and Jahaziel the priests regularly blew the trumpets before the ark of the covenant of God. (I Chronicles 16:4-6)

Notice the underlined portions. The ark was in the midst of the tabernacle, even as Moses' tabernacle was in the midst of the camp. Then we see that worship happened right in front of the ark with loud music. Asaph, who played the cymbals, was the chief musician and I doubt that he played them quietly all the time. Asaph was also a psalm writer and many of his psalms are in the Bible.

DAVID'S PASSION TO BUILD A MAJESTIC DWELLING PLACE FOR GOD'S PRESENCE

Solomon built the temple, but it was actually a product of David's passion. David's passion reveals God's heart in a way that may be unrivaled by anyone else other than Jesus.

David desired to bring back the ark and he built a tent for it. He passionately wanted to bring the presence of God into the midst of the city, as we have already seen. David wasn't satisfied with the tabernacle that he had prepared for it. He wanted God's dwelling place to be so glorious and majestic that it would be a better representative of the awesomeness of God's presence.

One of my favorite scriptures reveals very clearly the heart and desire of David:

> Now David said, "Solomon my son is young and inexperienced, and the house to be built for the Lord must be exceedingly magnificent, famous and glorious throughout all countries. I will now make preparation for it." So David made abundant preparations before his death. (I Chronicles 22:5)

David often wrote about how much He loved God's presence in the Psalms. He so wanted God's house to reflect how wonderful His presence was to him. So he told the people that God's house "*must be exceedingly magnificent, famous and glorious throughout all countries.*" David wanted to make God famous and impress the whole world with the temple he desired to build for Him.

What a prophetic example David is to us who live under the New Covenant. God no longer dwells in a temple made with hands. God now lives in the midst of His people; He lives in our hearts and manifests His presence in our corporate meetings. Oh that all God's people had such a passion for His current dwelling place to be "*exceedingly magnificent, famous and glorious throughout all countries*!" And oh that we would work together like Israel did to make His dwelling place even more glorious than Solomon's temple!

FINANCING DAVID'S TABERNACLE

We don't know much about the cost of David's Tabernacle or how he paid for it. We can only assume it was a relatively simple tent and that David used the king's treasury to pay for it.

What we do know is that David prepared a lot of resources for Solomon's temple, the subject of the next chapter. David birthed the temple in his heart and took great delight in gathering the resources for the building stage.

The tabernacle, to David, was a temporary dwelling place. It was important to him to get the Ark into the capital city, and the tent was a quick way to provide a place for it. The Ark had always been in a tent, so it was a natural way to temporarily house it. David had a passion to display God's greatness and majesty, and he couldn't wait for the temple to be built.

But let's turn our attention to the temple itself and Solomon, who saw it completed.

EIGHT

SOLOMON

The first word that comes to mind when you think of Solomon's Temple may be "gold". Almost everything in this temple was made of gold or overlaid with gold. Every building stone was covered with pure gold and most of the objects in the temple were made of pure gold.

FINANCING THE TEMPLE

This glorious temple probably was more expensive to build than any building in the history of man. At today's value, David's contribution would have been over $200 billion dollars in gold alone. There were also huge amounts of silver, expensive wood and precious stones. When you consider the labor for digging and shaping the stones from the rock quarries and for the intricate carvings and artistic works throughout, it's very obvious that this was one very expensive house for the presence of God.

Note the following example of the labor resources that went into the stone structure:

> Solomon selected seventy thousand men to bear burdens, eighty thousand to quarry stone in the mountains, and three thousand, six hundred to oversee them. (II Chronicles 2:2)

This labor force totaled 153,600 men. It did not include those who covered the stones with gold, hauled lumber, or did artwork or sculpting in the temple.

As we mentioned, David prepared an incredible amount of resources for Solomon. But Solomon continued to bring in more and more gold and silver into his kingdom from other nations, along with cedars from Lebanon and precious stones from various countries. Kings and queens came from other nations to see the temple and brought treasures from their own wealth as gifts for Solomon.

We don't know how much of that wealth went into the temple, but it was probably significant.

What we do know is that this temple was basically financed by King David and King Solomon. We have no record of the people bringing their jewels, etc., like they did in Moses' day. We also don't have a record that the people gave tithes to build the temple. This glorious temple was so expensive that only the king's resources could provide for it. We will see in the following chapter how this set a precedent for the restoration temple.

SPIRITUAL GIFTS IN OPERATION

We saw in a previous chapter that God had filled certain people with His Spirit to equip them to design and create many beautiful and artistic things in Moses' tabernacle. The spiritual gift of wisdom was the gift spoken over many of these creative people. Now that we come to Solomon's temple, we see the same basic spiritual gift come into play again.

First David, in giving a charge to Solomon, declared these words:

> Only may the Lord give you wisdom and understanding ... (I Chronicles 22:12a)

Then we read that God asked Solomon what he desired from Him. Solomon asked for wisdom and knowledge in II Chronicles 1:10. In I Kings 3:9, we read that Solomon asked for an understanding heart to judge God's people.

Putting both scriptures together, we see that Solomon desired what his father had prophetically charged him to receive. Here is a beautiful example of a son receiving a prophetic inheritance from his father. It's an example of the older generation imparting prophetically to the younger generation.

Both wisdom and knowledge are spiritual gifts listed in I Corinthians 12:8-10. Solomon was given an extreme portion of both of these gifts, and they were used not only in building the temple but in fulfilling Solomon's call to be the leader of God's people and to be a powerful testimony to the whole world of the greatness of God.

Sadly, even though Solomon had so much wisdom and knowledge, he failed to maintain the intimacy with God that David had enjoyed. Both of them sinned, but David repented because he couldn't live without the intimate relationship with God. Solomon, on the other hand, hardened his heart and apparently trusted in his own resources to finish his reign.

The nation soon began to suffer and eventually the beautiful house that he built was destroyed by invading armies. Sin first conquered the heart of a king and then destroyed the nation. Finally, the temple lost its glitter and glory and God's house was broken, just as God's heart had been broken. Without a home in the hearts of His people, He had no need for a house to dwell in, no matter how extravagant it was.

THE WORLD IS DRAWN TO THE GLORY

In Moses' time, the world discovered the greatness of the Hebrews' God when they heard about the plagues that He had placed on Egypt and how He had delivered His people from the greatest power on earth. In Solomon's day, the world learned about the majesty of Jehovah through the fame of Solomon's temple and his reputation for incredible wisdom and knowledge.

We are told that people came from far and wide to see the temple and to hear Solomon's amazing wisdom. The Queen of Sheba is the most famous visitor, as we are given some details of her trip. The Queen of Sheba thought others had exaggerated Solomon's greatness, but she declared that it was actually far greater than anyone had told her when she left. Thus the fame of Solomon's temple and his greatness spread from the palace to the peasant, and the whole world learned about the God of the Hebrews.

The significance of this is that in the ultimate convergence we will see the fame of God's greatness in both these spheres – that is the sphere of God's power through the signs and wonders being displayed, and the sphere of the wealth and beauty of what God's people build through the Spirit of wisdom and knowledge.

THE MANIFEST PRESENCE OF GOD'S GLORY

One of the greatest events regarding the temple occurred when it was dedicated. Not only did God speak clearly to Solomon, declaring His "If My People" covenant with Israel, but God's manifest glory fell and filled the temple. The priests were unable to minister for the weight of God's glory.

There is nothing we anticipate with greater excitement in the coming great convergence than the widespread intense manifestations of the presence of the Living God, causing men and women everywhere to fall on their faces in a deep sense of awe and holy fear.

Truly, there was never a greater earthly symbol of the heavenly majesty of God than Solomon's temple. Nothing before Solomon or since his time has been comparable to it, but whatever glory the temple reflected, there is a greater glory coming in both the visible and invisible realms.

We are not quite finished with the Old Testament record of facilities that hosted God's presence. After Solomon's temple was destroyed, most of the people of the land were taken away into captivity. But in their bondage they once again cried out to the God of their fathers and once again, He heard their desperate cry.

NINE

THE RESTORATION TEMPLE

After seventy years of captivity, God moved upon Cyrus, the Persian emperor, who was in the first year of his reign. His amazing decree is copied from the book of Ezra:

> Thus says Cyrus, king of Persia; All the kingdoms of the earth the Lord God of heaven has given me. And He has commanded me to build Him a house at Jerusalem which is in Judah.
>
> Who is among you of all His people? May his God be with him, and let him go up to Jerusalem which is in Judah, and build the house of the Lord God of Israel (He is God), which is in Jerusalem.
>
> And whoever is left in any place where he dwells, let the men of his place help him with silver and gold, with goods and livestock, besides the freewill offerings for the house of God which is in Jerusalem." (Ezra 1:2-4)

What an amazing miracle! A Persian emperor hears the voice of God, and he acknowledges that God has given him all the kingdoms of the earth. God then commands this Persian emperor to build Him a house.

Once again we see God's passion to have a place where He can have fellowship with men and women. While His people were lamenting over the loss of their homeland and their temple, God was also obviously saddened by the fact that He had no place on earth where His people could meet with Him. Thus He moved upon Cyrus and commanded him to build a house for Him in Jerusalem.

The thing that impacts me the most here is the fact that it wasn't about the Jews returning to their homeland that took precedence, it was the fact that there was no temple – no meeting place for God and man. As always, God was concerned about relationships first.

FINANCING THE RESTORATION TEMPLE

As we can see in the passage from Ezra 1 quoted above, people were instructed to help their Jewish friends with financial and material support, as they returned to Jerusalem to rebuild the temple. The following verses are very encouraging, especially when we view them as prophetic of the days in which we live, when God is restoring the glory of His church to the glory of its earlier days. Read with understanding the next two verses:

> Then the heads of the fathers' houses of Judah and Benjamin, and the priests and the Levites, with all whose spirits God had moved, arose to go up and build the house of the Lord which is in Jerusalem.
>
> And all those who were around them encouraged them with articles of silver and gold, with goods and livestock, and with precious things, besides all that was willingly offered. (Ezra 1:5-6)

What thrills me is the fact that God had moved the spirits of those who were to go and rebuild the temple. If God could move their spirits in those days to restore what was lost, then surely He can move the spirits of men again to restore what has been lost by the church.

Not only did God move the hearts of those who were to go, He obviously moved the hearts of those who were to give. This is also encouraging as we look forward to the ultimate convergence, when people will be motivated to give as never before to expand the Kingdom of Heaven on the earth.

The rest of Ezra 1 records the contribution of King Cyrus, which included many valuable articles, such as gold and silver platters, basins, knives, etc., which had been taken from the temple seventy years earlier when Nebuchadnezzar conquered Jerusalem.

In Ezra 6, Cyrus added another part to the decree; he declared that the foundation of the temple was to be laid with three rows of heavy stones and one row of new timber. Then he made this significant statement:

> Let the expenses be paid from the King's treasury. (Ezra 6:4b)

Later, King Darius, who had succeeded Cyrus, issued a decree of his own:

> Moreover, I issue a decree as to what you shall do for the elders of these Jews, for the building of this house of God: Let the cost be paid at the king's expense from taxes on the region beyond the River; this is to be given immediately to these men, so that they are not hindered.
>
> And whatever they need – young bulls, rams, and lambs for the burnt offerings of the God of heaven, wheat, salt, wine, and oil, according to the request of the priests who are in Jerusalem – let it be given them day by day without fail, that they may offer sacrifices of sweet aroma to the God of heaven, and pray for the life of the king and his sons. (Ezra 6:8-10)

What a remarkable decree! Not only did Darius reinforce Cyrus's decree, but detailed the items that might be needed in the house of God.

Another significant point is the urgency that the work in the temple would not be hindered. To overcome the hindrance that financial lack can cause in expanding the Kingdom of God, the King has declared that He is going to finance His work to get His good news to the ends of the earth.

Often, when speaking to groups, I ask how many would be doing more with their lives to expand God's Kingdom if lack of finances weren't an issue. There are always many hands raised. People would do more missions and local charity work, and a multitude of other things for the Kingdom if they could afford to. The ultimate convergence will bring a huge shift in the area of provision from the treasury of the King of kings.

By the way, this same Darius was the king that had to throw Daniel in the lion's den, and he stayed awake all night worried about him. When Daniel survived the episode, Darius made the following amazing decree:

> I make a decree that in every dominion of my kingdom men must tremble and fear before the God of Daniel. For He is the living God, and steadfast forever; His kingdom is the one which shall not be destroyed and His dominion shall endure to the end. He delivers and rescues, and He works signs and wonders in heaven and on earth, Who has delivered Daniel from the power of the lions. (Daniel 6:26-27)

PROPHETIC INVOLVEMENT

One of the most significant elements of the Restoration Temple was the vital contribution of contemporary prophets. After the restoration process had begun, Cyrus died and a new king became the emperor. Enemies of the Jews appealed to the new emperor to stop the Jews from rebuilding the temple and the city. As a result, the progress was halted for a period of time. Enter the prophets of God:

> Then the prophet Haggai and Zechariah, the son of Iddo, prophets, prophesied to the Jews who were in Judah and Jerusalem, in the name of the God of Israel, who was over them.
>
> So Zerubbabel, the son of Shealtiel, and Jeshua, the son of Jozadak, rose up and began to build the house of God which is in Jerusalem; and the prophets of God were with them, helping them. (Ezra 5:1-2)

I love the word, "so" starting off verse. As a result of the prophetic exhortations, the leaders rose up to build the house of God again. I also love the fact that the prophets practiced what they preached and helped the leaders, not only with words, but probably also with hard labor.

In Haggai 1, you can read where the prophet Haggai exhorted the people to stop building their own houses and return to work on the temple.

By this time, Darius had become the next emperor. As we have already seen, Darius reviewed the decrees of Cyrus to rebuild the temple, and he issued his own decrees, which reinforced those of Cyrus and took them to a new level. So when the enemies of the Jews tried to stop them again, Darius let them know that the Jews had his blessing, and anyone who tried to stop them would be punished by death.

Even as prophets such as Haggai and Zechariah stirred up the people to build a dwelling place for God's presence, so in the coming great convergence, we will see, and in fact are seeing, a tremendous resurgence of prophetic activity, causing the people of God to rise up again and build that place of habitation for Jesus.

Now, enjoy the following verse, which reinforces the importance of prophetic ministry:

> So the elders of the Jews built, and they prospered through the prophesying of Haggai the prophet, and Zechariah, the son of Iddo. And they built and finished it, according to the commandment of the God of Israel, and according to the commandment of Cyrus, Darius, and Artaxerxes, king of Persia. (Ezra 6:14)

Here we see not only the value of the prophetic encouragement, but also the value of the favor of kings and leaders in high places. I would suggest that the coming convergence will abound with special favor granted to Christian leaders by secular leaders in governments, business, entertainment and every mountain of society.

GREATEST SIGNIFICANCE OF THIS TEMPLE

Although Ezra's temple would be built centuries before Jesus' coming, it was indeed the temple in which Jesus would preach the gospel of the Kingdom and heal the sick. His blood would be shed not far from this temple, and as the Lamb of God, He would take away the sins of the world.

In reference to the Restoration Temple, Haggai prophesied these powerful words:

> "And I will shake all nations, and they shall come to the Desire of All Nations, and I will fill this temple with glory, says the Lord of hosts.
>
> The silver is Mine, and the gold is Mine, says the Lord of hosts.
>
> The glory of this latter temple shall be greater than the former, says the Lord of hosts, and in this place I will give peace, says the Lord of hosts." (Haggai 2:7-9)

Obviously, the greater glory of the Restoration Temple was the fact that the "Desire of All Nations" had come to manifest His Father's glory in that temple. Jesus filled the temple with His glory when he healed the sick and proclaimed the good news of the Kingdom of Heaven coming to earth.

Not only would the temple be filled again with God's glory to a much greater degree than ever before, but His coming would bring peace. This was announced by the angels to the shepherds. Jesus was called the Prince of Peace, and his coming has brought peace to hundreds of millions of souls in the world. Our goal is to increase that number until we can say billions rather than hundreds of millions.

Here again we see the Father's heart anticipating another special encounter with man. He sent His own Son, as His representative on the earth, to His chosen people who had so many times broken His covenant. However, His covenant would be restored, and He would once again walk in the midst of His people. This would be the greatest example of God walking with man since the Garden of Eden, and to prepare for it, God moved on the hearts of two emperors and many Jewish leaders. They responded and the temple was finally finished.

Obviously, we've gotten a bit ahead of ourselves talking about Jesus ministering in the temple. When He came to earth, Jesus was first hidden in Mary's womb, and then He appeared in a stable in Bethlehem. That's where we need to go next. Stay with me – the journey gets more exciting the closer we get to the present day.

TEN

THE INCARNATION

The heart of God had been longing for several millennia for a deeper, more personal relationship with mankind. In His omniscience, God had a plan that would provide the solution to the sin problem and enable man to come into His presence in a new and wonderful way.

Through Jesus, God actually came to earth and walked with men and women, and He revealed His love and power to them to draw them to Himself. Jesus taught them about the Father's love and desire for them, and He then demonstrated that love and desire by laying down His own life. This final sacrifice would take away the sins of His people, not just the Jews, but those from every tribe and nation who responded to His outstretched arms of love.

THE ROMAN WORLD

As mentioned earlier, God orchestrated the convergence of many changes in the earth, so that in the fullness of time, He could present His Beloved Son to those He had created in His own image for His own purpose and glory. These changes facilitated the quick dissemination of the gospel into the whole world, even as the invention of the Gutenberg printing press would later facilitate the distribution of Bibles in the language of the people at the time of the Reformation, a time when people wanted to read the Bible for themselves like never before.

Before the Roman Empire, the Greeks had conquered the world under Alexander the Great. The Greeks were advanced in education and philosophy and made Greek the international language of commerce and education throughout the known world. This enabled the Greek text of the New Testament to be shared and read in all parts of the empire. Even the Old Testament was translated into Greek in what is called the Septuagint.

When the Romans conquered the Greeks and took over that empire, they improved transportation and communication, building roads connecting country to country and city to city. Since most of the known world belonged to them, and they had to move their soldiers from place to place quickly, they invested a lot of time and resources in building quality roads.

These transportation routes became highways for the evangelists taking the gospel to the ends of the earth. It would have been much more difficult to go into all the world as Jesus had commanded, if they had not had the Roman roads and the freedom to go from country to country.

Compare this with the current advances in world-wide transportation and communication. With satellites, the internet, cell phones, and other modern communication devices, the gospel can reach the entire world at the speed of light. With air travel, missionaries can now travel to any nation of the world in a twenty-four hour period. God has truly set the stage for an incredibly quick and efficient harvest season on the earth.

The Romans also developed a new way of killing prisoners – crucifixion. To completely fulfill the prophecies of Old Testament prophets, Jesus would have to be crucified. He bore the curse for us prophesied in Deuteronomy 21:23.

THE WOMB OF MARY

The Father's plan required His Son to be born as a baby and enter the world in a humble way to identify with humanity. Therefore He had to find a young virgin to nurture this baby in her womb. That chosen young virgin was Mary.

To prepare her for this unique and potentially humbling assignment, God sent His top Messenger Angel, Gabriel, to Mary. When Mary inquired how this could happen, Gabriel said, "The Holy Spirit will come upon you and the power of the Highest will overshadow you; therefore, also, that Holy One who is to be born will be called the Son of God." (Luke 1:35)

What a bombshell to unload on a young gal! Gabriel found Mary to be the epitome of humility and availability, and she simply replied, "Behold the maidservant of the Lord! Let it be to me according to your word." (Luke 1:32)

Two important points stand out immediately that relate to the subject of convergence. When God prepares the earth for His coming, he involves His Messenger Angels. From our observation, their activity has been on a steady rise in the last number of years. More and more Christians are having angelic encounters; even unbelievers are being visited by angels who reveal Jesus to them.

The second point comes from the message of Gabriel. The Holy Spirit comes upon His people and overshadows those who will birth the new manifestation of God's presence on the earth. In the coming convergence, there will be many new manifestations of God's presence simultaneously birthed in different spheres and on different mountains of society.

Just as the Holy Spirit overshadowed Mary, He will overshadow many humble, little-known vessels to be used for His glory in the years ahead. Many of them will be young like Mary; some will be little children. Others will be faithful older warriors, who have served in the shadows and never received much recognition from the religious establishment. However, when the Holy Spirit overshadows these vessels, they will birth something so wonderful that the whole world will marvel, and God will receive the glory and honor and majesty He so rightly deserves.

THE INN

Located in Bethlehem, probably not far from where David kept his father's sheep, the inn, where Joseph and Mary spent that memorable night, had no normal room available for them. Thus, the expectant couple was sent to the lowly stable to give birth to the Creator of the universe.

To me, the Bethlehem inn represents the religious, political and commercial systems of our day. They relegate a visitation of the presence of God to a place on the fringe, not in the mainstream. They only want what seems respectable to them. Those in the mainstream can have good rooms at the inn, but those on the fringe can sleep in the stable.

THE MANGER

Jesus came to earth well under the radar of the religious leaders of His day, but the Holy Spirit and His angels were busy letting the shepherds and magi know what was happening, along with Zechariah and Elizabeth, Simeon and Anna. The shepherds were informed by a messenger angel and a large, enthusiastic entourage from Heaven that the Messiah was born in a stable, wrapped in swaddling clothes and lying in a manger.

I find it interesting that Jesus was placed in the manger – a feeding trough for the animals. The animals would probably eat the grain along with other food. Jesus would later declare that He was the Bread of Life. Bread, of course, is made from various grains. Jesus birth was thus prophetic of Him becoming food for the hungry.

But today, we, His disciples are His representatives and required to walk in His footsteps in many ways. Paul said, "For we, though many, are one bread and one body; for we all partake of that one bread." (I Corinthians 10:17)

As Jesus is the Light of the world, we are also called to be the light of the world. Since He is the Bread of Life, we are also called bread. Obviously, as Jesus fed the multitudes bread and fish, He will empower us to provide natural and spiritual bread and fish to the masses, especially in nations where there is great natural and spiritual hunger.

JOHN THE BAPTIST

Not only did God send His angels to prepare for Jesus' coming, He provided a second miraculous conception through Zechariah and Elizabeth, in order to have a prophet prepare the way for Jesus. Too old to have children, this priest and his wife were blessed in their old age with a special son who became known as John the Baptist. Here was a wonderful example of a servant; John the Baptist laid down his whole life and ministry to prosper the ministry of Jesus. He was willing to decrease so Jesus could increase. He denied being anyone important, but simply declared that he was nothing more than a "voice" in the wilderness to prepare the way of the Lord.

As Jesus prepares a sanctuary for Himself on the earth again, He will surely have other John the Baptist's to prepare for His coming. They will have the same servant's heart and will lay down their lives just as John did for Jesus.

SHEPHERDS AND WISE MEN

In spite of the hidden nature of the nativity, God made sure that Jesus had a special welcoming committee. God chose shepherds to be the first group of people to hear about Jesus' birth and to visit Him in the manger. Perhaps it was because David had been a shepherd and Jesus was to be called the "Son of David".

I do anticipate that in these days, we will see God reveal His surprises to those who have a true shepherd's heart. Not everyone we call "pastor", which means "shepherd" is truly a shepherd at heart, but God will share His secrets with those who truly love His sheep.

When the wise men arrived, Jesus was probably a toddler, living in a house in Bethlehem. Whereas the shepherds were already in very close proximity to the place where Jesus was born, the Wise Men, or Magi, as they are called, came from a great distance to honor and worship the King. These great men from the east brought gifts of great value, and these gifts were probably the means by which Joseph and Mary were able to travel to Egypt and back when Herod was trying to kill the young King.

As the popular saying goes, "Wise men still seek Him!" In the coming convergence, we will see many great leaders invest their time and money to get a glimpse of Jesus. There will be gold, representing God's glory, frankincense, and myrrh, representing our prayers and worship and His own fragrant presence.

BRUTAL OPPOSITION

Although God wanted Jesus to represent Him on the earth and He wanted to once again enjoy walking in the midst of His people, there was another reason for Jesus coming to earth. In order to provide the ultimate fix to the problem of broken relationships, Jesus would have to die as the Lamb of God, to take away the sins of the world. For that to happen, there would be those who would reject Him, and they would have to hate Him enough to crucify Him.

God used those religious leaders, whose hearts were full of pride and arrogance, to cause the crucifixion of Jesus. Just as God chose a humble virgin, simple shepherds, a number of eastern kings and others to bless the baby Jesus, He had to choose men with perverted hearts to cause the life-giving death of Jesus at Calvary.

When each player had fulfilled his role, the drama was complete. Today, we can all be beneficiaries of such amazing love on the part of the Father through His Son, Jesus. Through the working of the Comforter, the Holy Spirit, we can effectively share that same love with millions and billions of souls during the great harvest, which has already begun.

We could go on and on about Jesus' first coming to earth, but we have one more very important biblical historical record to examine. Before Jesus ascended into Heaven, He reminded His disciples that He would send the Holy Spirit, the Source of His power on the earth, to fill them and empower them to continue and expand His work on the earth. We want to now look at what happened when God came to inhabit His new and enlarged body of Christ on the earth.

ELEVEN

THE EARLY CHURCH

Now that the ultimate sacrifice and sin offering to God had been made, there was once again an opportunity for the God of Heaven to have a personal and intimate relationship with every man, woman and child on the earth. The first thing on God's agenda was to empower a small group of dedicated disciples.

God would His Holy Spirit upon them, baptizing them and filling them to overflowing. They would then carry the good news of the Kingdom of Heaven to the ends of the earth, and God would have many more children with whom He could fellowship and share His love.

PREPARING THE APOSTLES

A lot of space could be taken up on this subject, but simply stated, God took eleven diverse disciples, with lots of fleshly issues, and through His teaching and training, and allowing them to fail miserably, He transformed them into apostles of power and love. I don't think the church has really understood the significant impact that their failure at the cross had on them.

Just before the cross, the disciples were competing with each other for the most important spot in the Kingdom. After they forsook Jesus in His time of need, and after He had abundantly pardoned them and spoken, “Shalom!” to them twice, He commissioned them, saying, “As the Father sent me, so send I you!” The word apostle means, “sent one”. Thus, Jesus was not only forgiving them, but He was also graduating them from the “School of Discipleship” to the position of “Apostle of the Lamb”.

The disciples had failed their final exam, but were given an unforgettable lesson in grace. They had failed to take up their cross to follow Christ, and thus were unworthy to be disciples. But instead of rebuking or punishing them Jesus promoted them, sending them as His representatives to the ends of the earth. What a lesson in God’s amazing grace!

The disciples were thus emptied of their egos and were filled with loving passion for their Savior/Redeemer. Before the Holy Spirit fell in Acts 2, we find that there were one hundred and twenty saints waiting for the promise in an upper room for ten days. The amazing report is that they were all “in one accord.”

I believe one of the greatest miracles we will see in the near future, as a final preparation for Jesus’ return to earth, is God bringing His fragmented church from its present condition to a state of oneness. Jesus’ prayer in John 17 was answered then and I believe it will be answered again. There is no way that “the glory of the latter house will be greater than the former house” without the kind of unity that was so evident in the early church, as seen in the first few chapters of Acts.

THE POWER THAT PROPELLED THE EARLY CHURCH

The book of Acts is a book of miracles, signs and wonders. The miracles began with the initial baptism in the Holy Spirit, where prophetic tongues were spoken in the language of visitors to Jerusalem. Miracles were a basic staple of the early church, and those miracles were a powerful catalyst to explosive growth and multiplication. When the cripple, who had never walked in his life, was healed at the temple gate, the second great wave of converts was brought into the church. The number of men, which did not include family members, increased to five thousand. Conservatively speaking, this could mean a church with about twenty to forty thousand members.

The miraculous healings drew large crowds who gladly listened to the message of the Kingdom of God and about the salvation provided by the King for everyone who would receive it. The common people embraced this message, as they had Jesus, Himself. However, a religious opposition force that feared losing power and influence arose, and severe persecution was brought to the early church.

Although Jesus had already become the once-for-all sacrificial Lamb of God, the persecution and martyrdom of the early church kept it at a higher level of purity. The sincerity of the apostles was proven, and their witness that Jesus had risen from the dead was vindicated. Most men will not knowingly lay down their lives for a lie.

At that time, people didn't join the church just because it was the popular thing to do. Those who joined the church were really committed to their King, and they were willing to die for Him just as He had died for them.

This high level of purity helped maintain the church's power and influence for a long period of time. Later on, without the persecution, the church was still able to expand its influence world-wide, but its doctrines became corrupted and its supernatural power was severely diminished.

THE REVERENTIAL FEAR OF THE LORD

When the power and presence of the Holy Spirit was still at a very high level in the early church, the saints in Jerusalem were given a very vivid illustration of how costly it could be to take God's power and presence lightly. In Acts 5, we are told the story of a certain couple named Ananias and Sapphira, who wanted to look good before the rest of the saints, like Barnabas and others had.

So Ananias and Sapphira sold a piece of property and then decided to keep some of the money while pretending that they were giving the whole amount. They probably didn't anticipate Peter asking them if that was the total sale amount. My guess is that they supposed that they could just lay the money at the apostles' feet and that people would assume that they were doing what Barnabas and the others had done.

It might have come as a surprise to Ananias that Peter, prompted by the Holy Spirit, asked the question, "Did you sell the land for this amount?" Ananias, possibly caught by surprise, lied and said "yes." He immediately fell dead at Peter's feet. Sapphira entered the meeting about three hours later and Peter asked her the same question. Not knowing what had happened to her husband, she also lied and suffered the same fate.

As a result, "Great fear came on all the church and upon all who heard these things." (Acts 5:11)

During God's special visitations on earth, He reveals the fact that He is all powerful and not to be taken lightly or treated with disrespect. When the great convergence occurs, I believe there will be many instances of His people being taught the reverential fear of the Lord. People will not carelessly touch the "ark" of God's presence and live.

FINANCING THE EARLY CHURCH'S EXPANSION

We already alluded to the fact that people like Barnabas sold possessions and brought the money to the apostles, but financing the early church was more than just a few wealthy people donating their resources. We have an excellent description in Acts 2 and 4. Notice the following Scriptures:

> Now all who believed were together, and had all things in common, and sold their possessions and goods, and divided them among all, as anyone had need. (Acts 2:44-45)

> Now the multitude who believed were of one heart and one soul; neither did anyone say that any of the things he possessed was his own, but they had all things in common.
>
> And with great power the apostles gave witness to the resurrection of the Lord Jesus. And great grace was upon them all.
>
> Nor was there anyone among them who lacked; for all who were possessors of lands or houses sold them, and brought the proceeds of the things that were sold and laid them at the apostles feet; and they distributed to each as anyone had need. (Acts 4:32-35)

While it is obviously true that some had more to give than others, everyone did their part to provide for anyone who had a need. This is truly a case of supernatural love and generosity because no one was compelled to give. Yet because they were so overcome by the amazing love and grace of God, they were powerfully motivated to love others in response. The result was a church in which no one lacked anything that he or she needed.

The love and unity expressed in these verses seems totally unthinkable when we look at the church at large today, but what God has done before, He can surely do again. I have personally witnessed something somewhat close to this scenario. In 1973, while travelling with my mentor in Argentina, I witnessed the coming together of pastors who had not spoken to one another for months or years. When God began to pour out His Spirit and heal bodies and save souls, the pastors were overpowered by the love of God and repented of their hardness of heart.

When God can humble the leaders of the church, He won't have any difficulty with the people. I speak as one who is also a leader, and I know that it has almost always been the leaders who have squelched revivals throughout history. Leaders do have sincere concerns about their people getting caught up in false teaching or an impure movement. As leaders though, we are often suspicious of others out of fear that our own ministry might suffer. What happened to John the Baptist could happen to us. After John gave Jesus a resounding endorsement, his disciples began to leave him and follow Jesus instead.

INCREDIBLE JOY

Jesus had told His disciples that He was giving them His joy, so that they would experience fullness of joy. This was visibly fulfilled in the early chapters of the book of Acts. There was so much joy that they even counted it joy to be beaten and persecuted for Jesus.

That joy and enthusiasm came from the power and presence of God in their midst, and it was what propelled the church into such explosive growth. The formula for expanding the Kingdom of Heaven on the earth goes something like this:

1. Our own failure reveals our need of a Savior.
2. His abundant pardon creates passionate love for Him. He who is forgiven much loves much. (Luke 7:47)
3. Our love produces worship.
4. He inhabits our worship with His presence.
5. When He comes, He manifests with miracles.
6. Miracles bring great joy, as does His presence, even without miracles.
7. People are longing for joy, and those who have it, can't hold it to themselves.
8. Joy spreads like a virus from person to person.

And there you have the formula for expanding the Kingdom of Heaven on the earth.

This is what I expect to happen over and over again to bring in the great harvest. When the dead are raised to life, and every type of disease is cured, the joy waves will become tsunamis that sweep across the oceans to every tribe and nation under the heavens. I can hardly wait!

Once again, we could write almost endlessly about the amazing and powerful move of God that propelled Christianity into a world-wide movement. But we must move quickly now to address some of the times when God visited planet earth since those days. We will also learn a few things from those revivals.

TWELVE

VISITATIONS SINCE BIBLICAL TIMES

Under the rule of the Roman emperor, Constantine, Christianity spread quickly around the world. Sadly though, the purity and power of the gospel were greatly compromised and diluted. Unbelievers from many different pagan religions were compelled to convert to Christianity, but they were allowed to modify it to accommodate their own customs and religious practices.

Once again, the majority of those who called themselves the people of God were religious, but they lacked the intimacy and fellowship that the Father longed for from His people. Instead, the church became much like backslidden Israel under the Old Covenant. The people went through religious motions, hoping to gain Heaven and avoid hell, but very few knew how to bring pleasure to the Father's heart through intimate, loving worship.

Throughout those centuries, which have been called the Dark Ages, there were a number of exceptions. Certain mystics and monks pursued intimacy with God and kept the coals glowing, waiting for the days when the Wind of the Holy Spirit would once again fan the flames of revival on the earth.

THE REFORMATION

When you study the condition of the church before the Protestant Reformation, you can only shake your head and wonder how things got so bad when they started out so good. Instead of incredible power, authority and boldness with exhilarating excitement over the latest miracle healing or demonic deliverance, there was almost no power to heal or set captives free. Instead of generous and joyful giving to propel the Kingdom into the whole world, there was corruption, salvation by works or payment of indulgences to get relatives out of hell or purgatory. Instead of holy passion, intimacy with God and lavish love among the brethren, there was a lot of religious manipulation of the people, legalistic and religious ceremony, and political control.

The church of the dark ages looked very little like the church in the early chapters of the book of Acts. The church that had once set people free was now putting them in bondage. Just like the people of Israel had done in the Old Testament, they had forgotten God's goodness and served Him just like the heathens served their gods – out of fear.

The saddest part was that such a high price had been paid to restore a loving relationship that God no longer enjoyed. The blood of Jesus had been shed so that God could receive the love He craved from His creation, but so few men and women realized how much He wanted to be their Friend and dwell among them.

As always, God had a plan to fix the problem, and it began with the Protestant Reformation. It isn't necessary to go into specific details of the Reformation and its leaders, including Martin Luther, John Calvin, John Knox, etc., which is readily available on the Internet and in many books and movies. However, what the Reformation accomplished in regard to restoring God's intimate relationship with His people needs to be pointed out.

There is a very significant passage in the book of Acts where Peter is preaching to the crowd that had gathered in response to the lame man being healed at the gate of the temple. These verses are extremely pregnant with meaning:

> Repent therefore and be converted, that your sins may be blotted out, so that times of refreshing may come from the presence of the Lord,
>
> And that He may send Jesus Christ, who was preached to you before,
>
> Whom heaven must receive until the times of restoration of all things, which God has spoken by the mouth of all His holy prophets since the world began. (Acts 3:19-21)

The word "times" is translated from two different Greek words. The phrase "times of refreshing" uses the Greek word "kairos". Among other things, it means "a set or proper time, an occasion, or an opportunity". Here the word "refreshing" means a "recovery of breath or revival."

The word "times" is used twice, and it is obviously plural, referring to more than one occasion. In verse 19, Peter was not only referring to the time they were currently in, but also to future occasions or special set times when God would move on His people and refresh them with revival, or recovery of their spiritual breath. The word breath, wind and spirit are the identical word in the Greek – pneuma. Therefore, Peter was inviting them to receive the spiritual life being offered now, through the move of God in the early church, the appointed season for revival.

Peter was also saying that there would be other times in the future when God would move and bring revival to His people. The Protestant Reformation was certainly one of those times.

In verse 21, the "times" refers to the restitution, restoration or reconstitution of all things. Peter says that the heavens must receive Jesus until the times (plural) of the restoration of all things. The word "times" means spaces of time or periods of time. Here the Greek word "chronos" is used, from which the word "chronological" is derived. In other words, Jesus would stay in Heaven until the periods of times have occurred in which all things lost are restored.

Again, we see that this was one of those periods of time in which things were being restored. In itself, the Reformation certainly did not restore all that was lost since the beginning of the dark ages. However, the foundation, which would allow God to enjoy intimate fellowship with man once again, was laid. As long as man had to work for his righteousness, there was a wall between man and God; however, when the people learned that it was by grace through faith, that wall came down.

The history of the Reformation is not only a story of pain and suffering but of confrontation and conflict. People were imprisoned, burned at the stake, and forced to leave their homeland to follow their conscience. Every attempt to reform the church brought persecution and angry opposition. The messengers of the good news of God's grace were once again violently attacked by those who wanted to hold on to their position of power and wealth.

THE RENAISSANCE

The word "renaissance" means rebirth, and many things were reborn and restored during this period that paralleled the Protestant Reformation. The Gutenberg printing press not only facilitated the printing of Bibles in the language of the people during a time when people wanted to read the Bible for themselves like never before, but it also spurred on the advance of the arts and sciences.

It was a period of time where God was breathing on man's creativity and awakening the sleeping giant of spirituality. Larry Randolph, a well-known prophetic teacher of today, says, "The absence of creativity is the spirit of religion." The spirit of religion reigned throughout the dark ages, which drastically stifled the creative spirit.

When the Reformation converged with the Renaissance, a flood of creativity was released. New songs emerged with each wave of the Reformation. New art depicted the discovery of a new depth of spirituality. New discoveries in math and science often gave credit to the Creator for His marvelous work in creation.

Thus, the times of refreshing and restoration had begun, with many more times to follow. Each successive occurrence brought God closer to man and man closer to God. And every such event has thrilled His heart!

VARIOUS NEW MOVEMENTS

The times of refreshing and restoration continued throughout the centuries following the major upheaval known as the Protestant Reformation. The more the people were allowed to read the Bible for themselves, the more they found situations in the churches that didn't seem right. New leaders began to shine the light on truths that had been long neglected, and there was a desire to explore the Bible more and more.

ANABAPTISTS

During the Protestant Reformation, a number of groups began to proclaim the need to baptize converts rather than babies, and they insisted on immersion rather than the common practice of sprinkling. Those who baptized adults, who had been previously baptized as babies, were called Anabaptists (again baptized). Many groups later dropped the prefix and were simply called Baptists. As expected, those who were still sprinkling babies began to persecute the Anabaptists.

One group of Anabaptists, known as the Mennonites, was led by a man named Menno Simons. The Mennonites fled German Prussia to Holland to escape persecution by the Lutherans. Persecution followed them to Holland and they fled to Russia. As long as they didn't try to convert the Russian people, Catherine the Great granted them freedom of religion. They prospered in Russia and splintered into many divergent groups such as the Amish and Hutterites, along with the more mainstream evangelical Mennonites, from which my parents were born and raised. Their lives in Russia were thrown into upheaval by the coming of the Bolshevik Revolution – the beginning of the Soviet Union. Mercifully, many of them were allowed to leave Russia and migrate to the USA and Canada, as well as many other western nations.

It was interesting to discover that some of the Anabaptists were very much into charismatic phenomena and the necessity of using spiritual gifts, such as speaking in tongues, prophecy, healings, etc., as the Bible describes. There were many cases of major miracles, including the raising of the dead. For more details, one just needs to check Wikipedia on the Internet under Anabaptists.

As more and more doctrines came in line with Scripture, God was able to break through the barriers of ignorance and visit those who had hungry hearts. There were many more visitations to come, but at least there were now many who knew that God was looking for a personal commitment to discipleship, which involved a personal relationship with Him.

HOLINESS MOVEMENT AND THE GREAT AWAKENINGS

After the Anabaptist movement had spread throughout the world, God raised up John and Charles Wesley in England and John Whitefield in America to once again call people to a closer walk with God. It was the beginning of the Holiness movement and the First Great Awakening, which took place in the mid 1700's. It took man's personal relationship with God to a new level and stressed the need for man to live a pure life in order to be close to His God.

The fruit of this was far-reaching. Both the Wesley's and John Whitefield were involved in the Great Awakening in America, which prepared the way for the American War for Independence. Unknown to most Americans, one of the main reasons for the Revolutionary War was that many American leaders were against slavery, but the King of England was forcing it on them. Slavery was mentioned many more times than taxes in early American documents as a reason for separation from England.

John Wesley was actually one of the first preachers to oppose slavery, and his influence in America was quite significant. In those days, preachers had great impact on government and how people voted. The people expected their pastors to have wisdom as to how they should vote, since they were usually the most educated leaders in their communities. Thus, what Wesley preached made a significant difference.

DIVING HEALING

Although there were various instances of supernatural occurrences throughout the centuries following the Protestant Reformation, there was no large or sustained movement with an emphasis on the miraculous until later in the 1800's. Many Protestant denominations had officially adopted the doctrine of Cessationism, which declared that all the major miracles and spiritual gifts had ceased and were no longer needed or available to the church. They based these doctrines on the fact that we now had the Bible, and miracles were not needed like they were when the church was first starting out without any completed New Testament Scriptures.

However, in the late 1800's, men like Albert B. Simpson and Alexander Dowie began to preach and practice the doctrine of divine healing in the atonement. They attracted thousands of followers and the healing movement began.

Simpson started a Missionary organization known as the Christian and Missionary Alliance. He was also a prolific author, teaching about the need for a baptism in the Holy Spirit for holy living, as well as the doctrine of healing in the atonement.

Dowie had so much success in Chicago that city officials insisted that he get a license for practicing medicine, which he refused to do. He was fined daily until he left Chicago and started his own community named Zion, just north of Chicago. We have ministered on several occasions in the house where he lived a century ago. John G. Lake, whose family members had been dying off like flies, came to Zion to learn from Dowie. The result was another amazing healing ministry, and a new missionary-focused Pentecostal denomination.

This healing movement was another one of the "times" of refreshing and restoration, in which God was able to demonstrate, in a little stronger way, how much He loved the people whom He had created for His own pleasure. Many more seasons of refreshing were to follow and the best is yet to come.

THE PENTECOSTAL MOVEMENT

From a humble beginning in Topeka, Kansas, to an explosion of spiritual renewal in Los Angeles, the early 1900's saw the outpouring of the Holy Spirit with the gift of tongues manifesting in amazing ways. Soon the news of the Azusa Street Revival was spreading around the world, and the experience was replicated in city after city and meeting after meeting.

Out of this revival, many Pentecostal denominations were formed. Many of those who experienced this revival were from denominations that rejected the Pentecostal experience. This caused serious conflict and division in the church, just as it had in the Reformation and subsequent movements. Of course, no one was burned at the stake, but some were excommunicated from their churches if they practiced speaking in tongues or taught divine healing. My parents, who embraced the Pentecostal experience, were among those excommunicated by their Mennonite Brethren church.

THE LATTER RAIN MOVEMENT AND THE VOICE OF HEALING

In the late 1940's, in North Battleford, Saskatchewan, Canada, a series of events led a group called Sharon Schools to teach the doctrine that all five of the ministries mentioned in Ephesians 4 were to still operate today. These ministries were the apostle, prophet, evangelist, pastor and teacher. At that time, only the evangelist, pastor and teacher were recognized as valid ministries. Apostles and prophets were the foundation of the church, and theologians interpreted that to mean that they were there for the beginning, but were not needed any longer, since the foundation of the church had already been laid.

This group felt like their movement was spoken of in the prophetic Scriptures referring to the early and the latter rain. They also felt that God was pouring out His blessing for the last days by restoring the apostles and prophets to the church. They appointed one of their leaders as an apostle, another as a prophet, and so on. They didn't promote anyone else in their group, thinking only one of each was needed, but they did restore the concept that all five ministries were still for today. My own parents served in their Bible School when I was about four years old. We stayed there about two years and most of my earliest memories come from there.

Prophetic ministry was also encouraged by the group, as well as singing the Psalms and other Scriptures during the worship times. While this was happening, another movement converged with this one. A number of notable healing ministries began to arise, some of them with remarkable gifts of knowledge.

Information from the Holy Spirit would be given to people, like William Branham, concerning those they were to pray for. As I child, I witnessed him telling people their address, their phone numbers, birthdays and other uniquely personal information. He would also tell them what their sickness was and then he would pray for them. Many would be healed and the crowds would be amazed.

Soon there were many other healing ministries with evangelists like Oral Roberts, Jack Coe, A. A. Allen, T. L. Osborn and Gordon Lindsay. Many had huge tents and thousands would come wherever they went. They would see cancer tumors fall off, blind eyes see and deaf ears hear. Gordon Lindsay, joined with the others and published a magazine called "The Voice of Healing".

The healing movement lasted about a decade. According to some, God withdrew the healing anointing when it was abused by many healing evangelists. The spirit of pride and competition, along with other carnal problems had entered and defiled this movement. Since that time, we have never seen anything comparable in the western world to what we saw in the late 1940's and 1950's.

The healing movement of the mid 1900's did open the minds and hearts of many Christians to the fact that God loves people enough to heal them and that His power is still available today. Probably hundreds of thousands of people were healed during that time period and their testimonies were heard by multitudes more. The good news that Jesus still heals was out of the bag, and those who were honest with the facts believed it.

THE CHARISMATIC MOVEMENT

Not long after the Voice of Healing movement, the Holy Spirit began to fall on a number of traditional denominations, including the Episcopalian, Roman Catholic, Lutheran, Presbyterian and Methodist churches. Many of their members began speaking in tongues, prophesying, praying for the sick and acting much like Pentecostals. Many of these denominations wisely allowed those affected by this movement to remain in their churches, and special meetings were held just for these activities. There was certainly some opposition, but there was also compromise as well.

This movement spread world-wide, and there was a convergence with what was called the "Jesus People" movement. This was a revival among the youth of America, with many of them coming out of the drug and hippie culture. They began to relate to Jesus as a friend and One who had amazing power. He was One they could relate to, and through that relationship, they could actually experience something better than drugs and alcohol.

These convergent movements did much to shift the mindset of the church toward the fact that God wanted to be known by people in an intimate way. These movements allowed human feelings to be involved in such a way that they also converged with theological beliefs and spiritual sensitivity. God was thus warming His people up for the approaching ultimate convergence when He and His bride would co-inhabit the earth and Heaven.

THE FAITH MOVEMENT

Not long after these movements, the Faith Movement (also known as the Prosperity Movement) was born. Many preachers in the 1970's and 1980's began to proclaim the importance of faith, sowing and reaping and personal prosperity. Although, like other movements, there were extremes and teachings that lacked biblical balance, this movement also served its purpose in the greater plans of God.

The faith and prosperity movement challenged the predominant poverty spirit in the church, and brought balance to the issue of the church's attitude regarding finances. Because God would have to prosper His people for them to fulfill His plan for bringing in the harvest, they would have to get over those feelings that one couldn't be wealthy and still be humble and spiritual.

This movement did not focus as much on intimacy with God and fulfilling His desire for personal relationship as some of the later movements. It focused mostly on getting what you needed from God for yourself. This seemed to be a rather self-centered focus to many of us, but it did help the church get over its poverty mentality, which was essential to the purposes of God.

THE PROPHETIC MOVEMENT

By the 1980's, prophets were being acknowledged by a larger portion of the church of Jesus Christ. This restoration movement, led by leaders such as Dick Iverson, then pastor of Bible Temple of Portland, Oregon, began training people in personal prophetic ministry. The most common type of prophetic ministry prior to this was the congregational word, usually delivered in King James English, and often given in more traditional Pentecostal churches. People would stand up and speak words of exhortation to the whole group. This type of prophecy seldom released particular words of knowledge, but these prophecies were usually very general and often repetitious.

The new prophetic ministry featured personal words to people that included much more personal information, such as pain they had experienced in the past and things that would take place in their future. Prophets revealed and affirmed spiritual gifts, and their ministry encouraged wounded soldiers to rise up and fight again.

In 1982, the church we served in Oregon was blessed to have three prophetic elders come from Bible Temple in Portland to give personal prophecies to many of our people. We were asked to fast for three days to prepare our hearts before they came. After worshipping for awhile,

Brenda and I were seated in two chairs while the three prophets moved around us and prayed and prophesied one by one over us. It was one of the outstanding spiritual events of our lives. I wept profusely as they spoke things they had no way of knowing over my life. My wife responded in a similar manner. I still have the cassette tape and it has been an encouragement over the years.

This movement has spread through many streams and continues today. The prophetic ministry has done as much as anything else I know of to prepare men to know God in an intimate way. As a result of personal prophetic ministry, so many lives have been relieved of guilt and condemnation and touched by the Father's love. It also prepared the way for the next spiritual wave of the Holy Spirit.

THE APOSTOLIC MOVEMENT

The next wave followed quickly. It was the apostolic movement of the 1990's. The church began to embrace the concept that there really were apostles in the church today. These apostles needed to function in the authority God had given them if the church was to have the power and structure God needed it to have.

The prophetic movement had to come first or the apostolic movement would not have been accepted, nor would it have had the balance it needed. Apostles need prophets to affirm them, as they did for Barnabas and Saul in Acts 13. Prophets need apostles for balance and leadership to expand the Kingdom. The prophets had to come first, because they focused more on intimacy and personal relationship with God. This was necessary before apostles focused on power and structure. Without intimacy, this could have brought a very fleshly-type of power struggle among apostles.

The apostles and prophets are coming together today like never before, and they are laying a solid foundation for the great harvest. As they work in unity, they also empower the other five-fold ministries – the evangelists, pastors and teachers.

REGIONAL REVIVALS

The 1990's and 2000's featured a number of unusual regional revivals. In January, 1994, the Toronto Airport Vineyard, pastored by John and Carol Arnott, experienced a dramatic visitation with unique manifestations during special meetings with Randy Clark, another Vineyard pastor. Although highly criticized by large segments of the church, this revival ran six nights per week for several years and was attended by multitudes from every part of the world. After experiencing the impact of these meetings, pastors, leaders and lay people would return home and the same things would happen in their own churches.

Along with the more common phenomenon of falling under the power of God, the most signature manifestation was the "holy laughter". People would break out in uncontrollable laughter that was contagious to others, and meetings were in some ways like rowdy parties. Another typical manifestation was shaking or jerking, as if the person was being shocked with electricity every few seconds or so. In addition, many exhibited what they called "spiritual drunkenness", in which the person would slur and stagger and act like a happy drunk.

Naturally, this was not easy for traditional Christians to accept or approve of. Reports circulated of people barking like dogs, clucking like chickens, etc. Some of the manifestations did look and seem very strange and drew loud and strong criticism. However, the vast majority of those who were experiencing these phenomena were so filled with joy and so in love with Jesus, that no theologian could ever talk them out of it.

There were clearly people manifesting in the flesh, and sometimes the demonic was manifested as well. At the same time, many people were delivered from demonic powers, especially those of religious spirits. Every revival has had plenty of flesh and wild fire, but none were as analyzed, scrutinized and criticized as this one.

The meetings, which lasted several hours each, were filled with testimonies and demonstrations of God's power. Leaders were never in a hurry and there was no prepared agenda. People came to see the unexpected and they were never, never disappointed.

The most significant shift brought to the church through this revival was the awareness of God's desire to fill His people with exuberant joy and love. This awareness was necessary to counter the historic religious concept of piety - soberly serving God with sacrifice and suffering, without any joy. Jesus shared His own joy with His twelve disciples, so that their joy would be full. This joy will be needed when things in the natural world get more chaotic or fearful to many. His joy is our strength.

PENSACOLA, FLORIDA – BROWNSVILLE REVIVAL

On Father's Day, 1995, just a year and a half after the beginning of the Toronto Blessing, another powerful move of God broke out at the Brownsville Assembly of God in Florida when Pastor John Kilpatrick invited evangelist Steve Hill to speak. This revival saw some of the same manifestations as in Toronto, but it was also different in many ways. Because of the strong beliefs of its leaders, there was a much greater focus on traditional revival, along with the new phenomena. In other words, people were called to repent of many fleshly habits and practices, and Holiness was more emphasized in Brownsville than in Toronto.

Over the next five years or so, more than four million people visited this revival from all over the world. It also had a tremendous impact on the church world-wide. The church was awakened to see God as a personal and powerful God who could save, heal and set people free of every kind of weakness or addiction. Whereas Toronto had introduced a happy, loving God, Brownsville introduced the concept of a powerful, holy, and miracle-working God. I believe the order was also ordained by God. We need to know God's nature and feel His love before we get too deeply into the power dimension. Power can be dangerous if not controlled and motivated by love.

OTHER RECENT IMPACTING MOVEMENTS AND MINISTRIES

I will surely miss some of the significant movements and ministries, but I'd like to bring us more up to date by adding a few now. These are not necessarily numbered in order of importance, but each of these movements has had a real impact on the church and has helped prepare her for the great harvest.

1. Iris Ministries, under the direction of Rolland and Heidi Baker have brought about a major shift in the way people look at missions. Heidi has become one of the top-drawing conference speakers in the modern apostolic/prophetic movement. Her greatest passion is loving and hugging the poor, sick, blind, lame, and lost, one person at a time. Rolland and Heidi depend on unconventional mission strategies, which are shaking up the established modus operandi of missions.

   Instead of carefully planned strategies, they function on spontaneity, miracles and passion for Jesus and His presence. They have been impacted by and continue a close relationship with the Toronto Blessing leadership of John and Carol Arnott. After being "stuck to the floor" as she called it, for seven days in Toronto, Heidi returned to Mozambique and soon began to see the blind see, the lame walk and the deaf hear. For some time now, every deaf person she has prayed for in Mozambique has had their ears open, including those who were born deaf. Under their ministry leadership, the Baker's have also seen hundreds of people raised from the dead, food multiplied and many other miracles.

   Rolland also speaks at many conferences and is a great leader with numerous talents that help keep the ministry going. He is an excellent writer, photographer, bush plane pilot and also a brilliant theologian.

   The amazing results include untold multitudes of conversions, thousands of pastors trained, thousands of churches established, thousands of children taken in and cared for and hundreds of mission students who have been trained on the field. Additionally, hundreds of thousands of people have heard them speak world-wide and thousands also have gone to Mozambique and other mission bases to experience the revival themselves. I have made seven trips to their home base in Pemba, Mozambique, and I have taken many Americans and Canadians to visit and experience Heidi and Rolland in action. More information is available at www.irismin.org.

2. Another powerful ministry in our generation is based in Redding, California. Bethel Church, led by the teaching and healing ministry of Bill Johnson, has been sharing revolutionary and dynamic teachings with the church at large in conference ministry world-wide. Bill Johnson's teachings have transformed many thousands of individuals and Christian leaders. He has promoted an attitude of expectation for miracles in those who hear him, and he has developed a School of Supernatural Ministry, which has experienced exponential growth in the past few years. They have recently had to limit attendance and turn away more first year students than they could accept, because of lack of space. Students have come from far and wide to take the training.

   Bill Johnson has also authored numerous books with radical biblical concepts that help Christians shed their "dark ages" thinking and return to the way the church thought and acted in the first few chapters of the book of Acts. His book, "When Heaven Invades Earth" teaches one of his most revolutionary concepts. Based on a part of the Lord's prayer, "Your will be done on earth as it is in Heaven" Bill teaches that God wants us to pray down from Heaven the things we need on the earth, including health and provision, since there is no sickness or poverty in Heaven.

   But perhaps the most significant emphasis of Bill Johnson and Bethel Church is personal intimacy with God. Bill has experienced a very intimate relationship with God and has taught others to seek the same. As Heidi has affirmed many times, "All ministry flows out of intimacy." Bill will always put the presence of God before the miracles and ministry growth.

Bethel Church also partners with Iris Ministries in numerous ways. Recently, I heard both Heidi Baker and Bill Johnson speak at the same Asia for Jesus Conference in Taipei, Taiwan. I have heard them speak at other conferences together as well. Bethel has also raised support for Iris Missions and has helped with Iris administration in America. You can learn more about Bethel at www.ibethel.org.

Both Iris and Bethel have impacted hundreds of thousands of Christians to draw closer to Jesus and fall more in love with Him. The result is that more and more of the church is being equipped to participate in the coming harvest. The next ministry we will highlight is also impacting the world in a similar way.

3. International House of Prayer - IHOP - has also been on the scene for a similar period of time as the other two ministries just discussed. Led by Mike Bickle and a number of other dynamic young leaders and worshippers, this ministry is also multiplying world-wide and is especially impacting the younger generation.

This ministry has impacted some of our own children in a powerful way. The House of Prayer movement teaches the principles of the Tabernacle of David, which we have covered in an earlier chapter. The purpose of IHOP is to raise up a generation of prayer warriors, who not only pray in the traditional way, but also in a new style of prayer known as Harp and Bowl. This multi-faceted way of praying usually involves singing prayers and prophecies in various combinations of worship sets using apostolic and prophetic prayers from Scriptures, as well as people praying spontaneous prayers at the microphone in the prayer room.

When these Houses of Prayer become strong enough, they become 24/7 worship and prayer centers. The center led by Mike Bickel is located near Kansas City, Missouri, and has thousands of singers and musicians, who usually alternate with two hour shifts for each worship team. They have had continuous 24/7 prayer and worship for more than a decade at this writing.

In response to strong prophetic revelations, Mike Bickel's passion is to raise up this generation of prayer warriors. At the close of each year, he and his team host a conference called "One Thing", based on Scriptures such as the following:

"One thing I have desired of the Lord, that will I seek: That I may dwell in the house of the Lord all the days of my life, to behold the beauty of the Lord, and to inquire in His temple." (Psalms 27:4)

Between ten and twenty thousand passionate worshippers from the younger generation attend annually, and I believe that many of these will be the backbone of the coming worldwide harvest. More information is available from their website: www.ihop.org.

4. International Coalition of Apostles (ICA) is an organization of those recognized as apostles around the world. Founded by Dr. C. Peter Wagner, this loosely connected organization has brought together hundreds of apostles from a multitude of nations and has established some unity and consistency in Kingdom expansion concepts and leadership.

   This organization has now transferred leadership from Dr. Wagner, who felt called to semi-retirement at the age of 80, to Dr. John Kelly. Under Peter Wagner's leadership, this movement has focused on understanding what God was doing on the earth to expand His Kingdom. It has brought some balance, with a more intellectual or analytical approach, for charting the course of the church in these last days. The website for ICA is: www.coalitionofapostles.com

   Dr. C. Peter Wagner has been a prolific writer, and his concepts have given the church an understanding of the major issues facing the church, such as understanding the indispensable role of the apostle and how they relate to prophets.

> Another major focus has been the coming transfer of wealth, which is spoken of in Scripture and reinforced by many of the current prophets. This is one of the prophetic messages that we believe is extremely important for the propagation of the gospel of the Kingdom throughout the world. We will deal with this in much greater detail in our next chapter.

There have been many other great revivals and ministries that have positively impacted the church over recent years and decades. The ones mentioned are the ones that have captured my attention. Please forgive me if I have missed one of your favorites. Let's move on now to the most important chapter of all, where we will provide a prophetic picture into the days and years ahead. Nothing I can imagine could be more exciting than what we will now discuss.

THIRTEEN

THE GRAND FINALE ~ THE ULTIMATE CONVERGENCE

I am excited, yet cautious, as I come to this final chapter. I want to pass on a tremendous amount of excitement about the future, but I also want to be careful not to prophesy anything out of my own personal thoughts and desires. Neither do I want to take credit for what others have prophesied in my hearing. However, I am full of conviction that the things I will share with you now are true and will truly come to pass.

I have been very blessed to have become associated with a number of people who hear the Word of God very clearly and frequently in their spirit. I have also been in the company of others prophetic leaders, whom I know less personally, who have shared things that God has shared with them. The revelation that God has given me regarding the ultimate convergence of a multitude of entities in a simultaneous demonstration of shock and awe builds upon the many revelations that I have heard from others. With that little word of explanation, let's try to lay it all out now.

THE ULTIMATE PURPOSE OF GOD

Let's first remind ourselves of the "why" of this ultimate convergence. God's heart has always been and always will be to have intimate fellowship with those He created for that singular purpose. History is His story of how He desired and drew men and women to Himself and dwelt in their midst whenever their willing hearts would allow Him to.

Let Exodus 25:8 resonate forever in our hearts. God said, "And let them make Me a sanctuary, that I may dwell among them."

God's purpose for this ultimate end-times convergence is so that His people can build Him a sanctuary where He can dwell among them. We know, of course, that this is not just for His selfish desires. His desires as a Father are wrapped up in His abilities to bless His children with all of His goodness, which is the very highest win/win scenario. There are no greater extremes of joy than being in His presence and having Him around to provide for all the needs of our lives - body, soul and spirit.

THE COMING UNPRECEDENTED TRANSFER OF WEALTH

While I would rather talk about this later on in this chapter, I know that nearly every other entity in the ultimate convergence will be at least partially dependent on this event. Therefore, we will deal with it first to make the other events a little more believable to the reader.

A number of well-known and established apostolic and prophetic leaders have been speaking about a powerful transfer of wealth that will facilitate the world-wide harvest. In the fall of 2004, at a Kansas City conference, I heard the venerable prophet, Bob Jones, prophesy about God giving a brand new energy technology by revelation to a Christian businessman from a certain city. He talked about freedom from foreign oil within a short number of years.

Others, such as Dr. C. Peter Wagner, began teaching the biblical principles of the transfer of wealth from Isaiah 60 and other Scriptures.

Much of what was prophesied to the nation of Israel was also applied to the people of God, who could also be Gentiles.

Around the same period of time, a young prophet named Shawn Bolz had a visitation from an angel who identified himself as the "Minister of Finance". He informed Shawn that God was going to be delivering creative inventions and huge amounts of money to certain Christian men and women that He could trust to bring in the harvest.

Along with all these and many other prophetic pronouncements, I have been privileged to learn of things which I cannot yet publish, that make me extremely excited about the future. What I can say is that what is coming in the area of finances for the Kingdom harvest is going to be beyond the most optimistic hopes and dreams. What God did for Solomon to reveal His glory to the world will be replicated and expanded upon in such a way, as to catch the attention of the whole world.

Because of this immeasurable transfer of wealth into the hands of Kingdom-minded leaders, no Kingdom projects will be impossible or restricted for lack of finances. Instead, God will empower armies of creative conquerors, equipped to devastate a defenseless enemy and to set multitudes free to see and experience the awesome glory of God. Throughout this chapter, you will see how useful this transfer of wealth will become.

CONVERGENCE OF FINANCIAL PROVISION FOR THE TEMPLE OF GOD

With talk about the transfer of wealth and all the financial issues, we don't want to forget our primary focus, which is to build God a sanctuary on the earth in which He can dwell among us. That sanctuary is the expanded and united body of Christ around the world. It involves the harvest, because many members of His future body are not yet attached to Him. But It also involves uniting the current members of His body into a single, mature man (Ephesians 4:13), which will then be united with those who will be saved during the harvest.

As we recall the frequent occasions in the past, where finances were supplied for the tabernacles and temples, the people were sometimes asked to give free-will offerings to build the sanctuary and furnish it. In other cases, the king declared that it would be paid for by the King's treasury. When Solomon built His temple, there is no record that he asked the people to give. King David and King Solomon both gave enormous amounts of wealth from their Kingdom and King David gave from his own private stash.

I do believe that both of these scenarios will converge in the coming revival. Everyone will want to have a part in providing for the harvest. Many will sacrifice their vacations, retirement savings, extra properties, etc., in order to send the laborers into the harvest or to finance themselves on mission trips and other events. Some will want to support or help raise orphanages, provide wells or hospitals, etc.

As it was in the restoration temple of Ezra's day, the people were encouraged to give, but the King also authorized that all necessary expenses of the temple were paid from the King's treasury. There will be vast amounts of money supplied by the King of Kings through creative technology that He will release through those He can trust.

CREATIVE ARTS EXPLOSION

Just as we began in the Garden of Eden and the Tabernacle of Moses with God's creative beauty, we are going to see a brand new Renaissance and more in the area of the arts. It is something that will catch the arts and entertainment world completely off guard.

When Christians are suddenly making the greatest blockbuster movies with cutting edge technology, Hollywood will do a double take. When the best art in the world is produced by those with no professional training, but the artists testify that they have been to Heaven and are being taught by Jesus (like young Akiane Kramaric of Coeur D'Alene, Idaho), the world's artists will stand back in amazement, as will the rest of the world.

When God anoints artisans with the Holy Spirit, like He did in the days of Moses, to create unusual and deeply prophetic works of beauty for the world to behold, men and women will be brought to tears as God touches their hearts. When the moving of the Holy Spirit synchronizes dancers and musicians to gracefully and powerfully portray God's love and grace, the hearts and souls of men and women will melt before the God who loves them.

In addition to the anointing of wisdom and creativity, God will also provide the financing for the movie productions and the arts, which require large amounts of capital. Without the transfer of wealth, progress would be very slow, as it has been over the previous decades. When God fires up the wealth-transfer engine, these artistic developments will explode all over the earth.

SPIRITUAL PREPAREDNESS

Many Christian leaders are rightly concerned regarding this transfer of wealth. Over the course of church history, excessive wealth became a negative factor when it was used for self indulgence or as a means to control others rather than for the use of God's higher purposes. The good news is that God has already made plans to minimize this problem in His Kingdom.

The most exciting thing to me, as I travel in meetings throughout North America and the world, is the revival of passion and deep devotion for Jesus, especially among the younger generation, who will be the labor force of the coming great harvest of souls. With leaders like Heidi Baker, Bill Johnson, and Mike Bickle teaching them to be laid-down lovers of Jesus, they are more than willing to live and die for Jesus.

In this younger generation, there are many who love to spend hours in prayer and worship – something that the youth of my generation seldom considered. In those days, church and youth meetings were a mixture of a little spiritual stimulation and a lot of social activities. That still exists in some circles, but there is a completely new brand of deep, passionate worshippers, who have already paid a price for intimacy, who won't care about money, fame or fortune.

STADIUMS AND OPEN AIR MEETINGS

Some of the senior prophetic leaders in the church today have seen repeated visions of stadiums filled with mostly young people, led by half a dozen unknown youth. In these visions, these youthful leaders call out sicknesses, etc., through the word of knowledge, and people are getting healed all over the stadiums. The dead would be brought to these meetings and raised to life. The TV news reporters and cameras would be there, and they would report what was happening on the nightly news.

This would be happening all over our nation and the world. Sports activities would be cancelled because everyone wanted to be at the meetings. Bob Jones recently declared that the stadiums would become too small, and they would have to move to fields to facilitate the crowds. Bob Jones was also promised that he would see a billion youth come to God in an upcoming great revival that would occur in his lifetime; he foresees this word coming to pass very quickly.

When there is such a great move of God, few people will worry about money. Material possessions cannot compare to the exuberant joy of seeing amazing miracles – cripples walking, blind folk seeing, deaf people hearing and tumors dissolving, not to mention the dead being raised back to life. Nothing can compare with that, and those whom God entrusts with Kingdom Finances will want to expand the revival in every way possible.

UNITY IN CHRIST'S BODY ON THE EARTH

As Jesus taught us to pray, "Your Kingdom come, Your will be done, on earth as it is in Heaven". We must pray for unity in the church, which will require a greater miracle than the transfer of wealth into the hands of the church and the nation of Israel. Many Christian leaders have no faith or even hope that this could happen. They are so accustomed to a divided church, with theological chasms between denominations, that they cannot foresee the differences being overcome in their lifetimes or any time in the future.

I believe that this is one of the most important and boldest prophecies in this book, but I make it without any hesitation. The body of Christ will come together in a way that we haven't seen since Acts 1-5. Since there is no disunity in Heaven, and God told us to pray that His will would be done on earth as it is in Heaven, and since He's done it before in the early church, then I do believe He can and will do it again.

In order for the glory of the latter house to be greater than the former house, unity in the true body of Christ will have to happen. Denominational pride and jealousy will be overcome by the presence and power of Jesus among us. I saw it happen among many pastors of Cordoba, Argentina when the power and presence came. Proud leaders humbled their hearts and made things right because no one wanted to miss out on what God was doing.

When you see leaders of various movements tearfully confessing pride and jealousy relating to other leaders in the body of Christ, get excited. Greater things are coming! When you see a lot of it happening, you will know that revival has come to your city or nation or the world.

WORSHIP IN THE ULTIMATE CONVERGENCE CHURCH

It may not be easy to predict the styles and types of music and worship in the great harvest church, but God has already given us some clues. Let's look at one clear clue in the book of Acts.

"After this I will return and will rebuild the tabernacle of David, which has fallen down; I will rebuild its ruins, and I will set it up; so that the rest of mankind may seek the Lord, even all the Gentiles who are called by My name, says the Lord who does all these things." (Acts 15:16-17)

When James quoted Amos 9:11-12, he focused in on the fact that Gentiles were now receiving the gospel, but it also clearly indicated that the Tabernacle of David was being restored. As we have already seen, the Tabernacle of David was known for its thousands of skilled musicians and their continuous worship near the Ark of the Covenant. This is clearly a prophetic picture of the worship that is coming with this great and incredible move of God.

Remember that we are not just expanding God's Kingdom on the earth, but we are building Him a wonderful and magnificent house in which He can dwell. The Ark represented God's presence. As God's presence becomes more real and powerful in our midst, I believe we will see increasingly more intense worship, especially when the miracles start to happen in quick succession. At that time, worship will literally flow out of the hearts and mouths of hundreds of millions of worshippers.

A supernatural anointing will fall on musicians and vocalists. Angels will assist and contribute to the symphony. During worship, children and the aged alike will be touched by the presence of God. They will see visions, receive words of knowledge, and transfer the healing power of God into the bodies of the sick, diseased and mentally disturbed. Worship will change the spiritual atmosphere and even the natural weather will be affected. People will come to Christian gatherings and linger for days, not caring if they eat or drink, becoming so intoxicated with the presence of God that they experience no discomfort from fasting.

During times of worship, revelation and divine strategy will be released for building God's Kingdom and reaping the great harvest. Under the canopy of worship, people will be transported to other nations on special assignments. They will return and no one will even know that they had gone. It will be difficult for people to know if they had really gone in person or if they had just gone in their spirit man. Yet lives will be changed, bodies healed and relationships restored because of their mission from Heaven.

CONVERGENCE OF REVIVAL PHENOMENA

One could ask the question: "What will the revival meetings look like in the great harvest season?" A few years ago, I wrote an article called, "How Do You Measure Fire?" It was published on the Elijah List and in the Elijah Rain magazine. At the end of the article I prophesied what to expect in the revivals of the future. Here is that prophetic word:

I believe the Lord is proclaiming, "My fire will be kindled in many of the darkest places in the land. In the secret chambers of wickedness my fire will fall on desperate hearts. I will turn things inside-out and upside-down. Those who use ministry for personal gain, who have neglected the fire which I had put within them, will not see the favor which I will give to those who are now embracing the fire. But those who have been the last shall be first and those who have been first in their own eyes shall be last.

But revival fires will be carried back and forth across the oceans and across the deserts and across the plains and the mountains. Fires from the cities will be mixed with fires from the country. Fires from the north will be combined with fires from the south. The fires from the east and west will meet and my people will say, 'This is a fire which cannot be measured – it is too big and moving too fast.'

But I have already measured it, says the Lord. It has filled the Heavens and will fill the earth. This fire is given to empower my church to bring in the great harvest. This is a fire that will purify hearts, illuminate minds and empower the harvesters.

The fire will fill every willing vessel. There are many vessels which I could use, but I will use those which are full of the fire, not those whom man would choose.

And now, I command the fire to fall on the sacrifice that is on my altar. I decree that those who cry out for the fire will become blazing torches to light the way for many. They will open the doors to many hearts and even my prophets will say, 'We have not seen this before. Here are unknown vessels proclaiming the word of the Lord with fire and authority. Surely they have received the fire from Heaven.'

My holy fire will not be stopped by any human or devilish strategy. My fire will burn until I restrain it on the earth and all things are fulfilled. But today, embrace the fire, put yourselves on the altar and prepare to burn like the bush which Moses saw. As you burn for me, many will turn aside to see the fire that I have kindled. For you will burn, but you will not be consumed, for the fire in you is the fire of my great glory and it shall bring you incredible blessing." says the Lord.

The fire of God will manifest in a multitude of ways. Elements from every revival will converge to make these revivals incredibly exciting. No two meetings will look alike. People will fall under God's power, they will shake under the anointing and others will laugh with incredible joy. Some will weep in God's presence, while others will cry out for forgiveness for their pride and hardness of heart. Healings will break out without anyone touching anyone or even giving them words of knowledge.

THE MAGNIFICENT TEMPLE

As David declared in a previously quoted verse, "The house that is to be built for the Lord must be exceedingly magnificent, famous and glorious throughout all countries." (I Chronicles 22:5) Even so, the temple for God's presence in the great harvest church must be even more magnificent, famous and glorious. And of course, we the church are that temple. So what will this look like?

Both the Tabernacle of Moses and Solomon's Temple had incredible artwork and both had an abundance of gold, silver and precious stones. These first represent spiritual wealth, miracles, signs and wonders, and the glitter of God's glory, but we will also see a great release of material wealth to display God's glory to the watching world. This wealth will be used to develop movies using state-of-the-art technology, works of art and other things that will attract the attention of the world.

I am not saying that we will focus on material things. The focus will clearly be the power and love of God, but that will also converge with some examples of the wealth and creativity that God is giving to His people, His church, His bride. With this wealth and the creativity that it empowers, the church will be a sign and a wonder to the people who respect those things. God will be revealing that He can be all things to all men.

For those who admire great works of art, He will anoint and financially empower His gifted artists. For those who love music, drama and opera, God will anoint and financially empower the most creative musicians, actors and singers. For those who admire magnificent architecture, God will not spare the expense to build the most spectacular buildings.

If God could give David and Solomon hundreds of billions of dollars worth of gold, silver, precious stones, cedar and other building materials, He can do it again, only more so. The coming transfer of wealth will be much greater than people can even imagine at this time. There will be an abundance of finances to feed, clothe and educate the hungry. There will be funds to train and send a new generation of anointed missionaries into every part of the world. God will also provide some extravagant displays of His wealth.

I don't believe Heaven is a place where one has to be careful with money because of fear that there won't be enough to go around. Even so, we will be bringing the conditions of Heaven to earth through faith, which will work through love, which will increase as we worship before the presence of the Most High God.

THE SEVEN MOUNTAINS OF SOCIETY

We have alluded in previous chapters to the seven mountains of society, a concept made known in recent years by speakers such as Lance Walnau and authors such as Pastor Johnny Enlow. These seven mountains of society are the most important elements of society that control the destiny of its people. I want to prophesy some dynamic developments on each of these mountains, but before I do that, let me share a fresh revelation relating to these mountains. First let's look at a wonderful verse in Isaiah.

> Now it shall come to pass in the latter days that the mountain of the Lord's house shall be established on the top of the mountains, and shall be exalted above the hills. And all nations shall flow to it. (Isaiah 2:2)

Here is an amazing prophetic picture of what will happen when the dwelling place of God is established on the tops of each of the seven mountains and tower over them. From the Garden of Eden to the tabernacles, the temples, the early church and the restoration church, we have seen God come and take His place among His people, whenever they allowed Him to prepare Himself a place and cooperated with Him in the building.

But now we come to the place where God is preparing a place of high honor and glory. He wants His presence to be made known and to be seen by all the world by going to the tops of these mountains and building Himself a dwelling place there. The highest mountains are visible from a great distance and God wants the mountain of His house to be seen by the whole world. He wants them to know about His love and power and His desire to dwell among those He has made in His own image.

As I read the story of Abraham preparing to offer Isaac on the mountain, I was touched by the name that Abraham gave to the place on the mountain after he found the ram in the thicket. That ram was the sacrifice that God provided instead of Isaac. Please read the following verse:

> And Abraham called the name of the place, "The-Lord-Will-Provide; as it is said to this day, 'In the Mount of the Lord it shall be provided." (Genesis 22:14)

The last quote is what really ministered to me. Provision comes in the Mountain of the Lord. Provision – the transfer of wealth – will come to the people of the Kingdom when they meet with the King on His mountain. His mountain becomes His house – His dwelling place. It's the Father's House – the house which is a House of Prayer, where He makes His people joyful in His House of Prayer.

> Even them I will bring to My holy mountain, and make them joyful in My house of prayer. Their burnt offerings and their sacrifices will be accepted on My altar; for My house shall be called a house of prayer for all nations. (Isaiah 56:7)

I believe this is one of the most significant truths in this book and it is a theme which has been woven into every chapter. We MUST come together in unity in the Mountain of the Lord, worshipping Him together, enjoying His presence, just as He enjoys ours. We MUST love Him with all our hearts. We MUST allow Him to fill us with His joy. We MUST let Him empower us to rise up to conquer every mountain of society.

Why did Abraham go up the mountain? It was to meet with God and offer Him a sacrifice. And what did God provide on the mountain of the Lord? It was something that Abraham could offer up to God.

Here is a tremendously significant key in receiving the provision of the Lord on the Mountain of the Lord. Our provision is primarily for the purpose of offering it back to God. We do this by building His Kingdom with whatever He gives to us as we worship Him on the Mountain of the Lord. Of course, we get to enjoy everything He puts in our hands before we pass it on, and in addition, He keeps sending more and more wonderful gifts and blesses us with special personal treats as well. But He gives the most to those who have the biggest hearts – those who love to give to others and those who love His Kingdom and want it to grow like the mustard seed grows when planted in fertile soil.

God is a giving and loving God and those who spend time with Him become like Him. And when we become like Him, we become giving and loving people. When we give and love, He provides more for us to give and to show His love. It's a wonderful, divine cycle of life.

Let's go back now to the seven mountains. Here is what I believe God will accomplish on each mountain of society when this Ultimate Convergence takes place:

1. FAMILY

Through the influence of revival, God will heal broken families and restore relationships between the older and younger generations.

Divorces will be prevented and abortions will be avoided. Families will pray together again without being legalistic or religious about it. Prayer will be a natural reaction to good news or bad news, and praise and worship will fill homes. It will be a glorious development.

2. RELIGION

Churches will certainly be impacted by the revivals. Agendas and rituals will be abandoned in order to give the Holy Spirit the freedom to move as He desires. Pastors will reach out to other churches in their cities and offer to help them in various ways. They will work together on city revivals and reconcile previous differences. God will lead churches who have been focused on self-preservation and building their own ministries, and they will focus on building the Kingdom in their region, as well as in the whole world. Missions will prosper through their generous support.

3. EDUCATION

Christians will begin to rise up and bring change to the atheistic domination of education, which began many decades ago. Textbooks are already being adjusted and many are seeing the importance of what our children are being taught. Christian schools, colleges and universities will grow, but Christians will certainly also permeate the established secular schools. I also predict that a number of top educators will be converted during revival services, many of which will take place on their very campuses.

4. GOVERNMENT

God will continue to prepare His chosen vessels to run for the highest positions in government on every level. There will be angry opposition, but many will succeed in getting elected through the enthusiastic support of Christians who are listening to the voice of the

Holy Spirit, as well as by non-Christians who are looking for some honesty and integrity. They will see and discern the difference. These new-breed politicians will put moral issues before monetary issues, and they will save nations from disaster by procuring God's favor. Based on prophetic input from others, I personally expect a strong new political party to emerge in the United States, which will bring a quicker transformation of the federal government.

5. ARTS AND ENTERTAINMENT

As already mentioned, new anointings will fall on artists and artisans of all types. New styles of music will emerge through gifted men and women of God in Nashville, Hollywood and New York, as well as on secular and Christian TV stations. Christians will win talent awards and athletes will give glory to God for their gifts and help.

6. MEDIA AND COMMUNICATIONS

More Godly media outlets will arise, and Christians will learn new ways to use the Internet and other developing technology. There will be an increase in honesty and integrity, as Christians invade the media and develop new media. Corruption will be more quickly exposed in politics and business, and the media will fulfill its major function in society.

7. BUSINESS AND FINANCE

This is another mountain which, like the government mountain, will put up a huge fight against all who would climb their way to the top. Through the unfair advantage that God has given them with His revelation and creative inventions, they will leap-frog over many. This will come as a huge shock and annoyance to the current leaders who have been established in high places on this mountain for decades or even centuries. With a tremendous transfer of wealth going on, many leaders will slide quickly to the lower levels of this mountain, while Christians will be catapulted to the top. They will provide huge amounts of wealth to Kingdom projects of all kinds, resourcing leaders on all the other mountains.

For more information about these mountains, check out lance-learning.com, or books by Johnny Enlow, entitled "The Seven Mountain Prophecy" and "The Seven Mountain Mantle". You can also check our website: kingdomsendingcenter.com for two of my books, entitled, "Kings and Kingdoms", and "Finding Your Place on Your Kingdom Mountain."

WRAPPING UP

It should not be necessary to detail every item that was highlighted, as we looked at the different times when God came to dwell among His people. To conclude this final chapter, let's go back to the questions that were asked near the beginning of the book and answer them:

Yes, I do believe that there will be an amazing ultimate convergence of many powerful and positive influences at the same time.

Yes, I do believe there will be amazing and fruitful unity in the body of Christ once again.

I do believe there will be a generation with a great and passionate desire to serve the King.

I believe there will be a huge transfer of wealth from the godless to the godly, in order to equip and send a godly generation into the harvest fields of the earth.

I believe there will be a huge renaissance of Christian art, drama, music, literature, movies, etc.

I believe there be Christians who discover new technologies and develop inventions that help solve the major problems on planet earth.

I believe there will be Christians developing new medicines and discovering health secrets that will give people a much longer life with a better quality of life at the same time.

Most importantly, I believe there will be a restoration of the glory and power of the early church with signs, wonders and miracles, producing wave after wave of souls coming into the Kingdom.

I also believe the church will multiply and find favor with God and man.

I believe that many people will be transported like Philip.

I believe there will be an increase in major creative miracles and the raising of the dead.

I believe there will be a great resurgence of angelic activity.

I believe that people will have greater and more frequent visions, dreams and Heavenly visitations.

I believe there will be revivals of repentance like there were in the Great Awakenings.

I also believe there will be revival phenomena like the outbreak of laughter, shaking, falling and apparent drunkenness.

I believe there will be signs and wonders like gold dust and feathers falling from the ceiling, etc.

I believe people will be anointed, like Joseph and Daniel were, to rise up and take political leadership positions in the world.

I also believe they will be able to reduce injustice, suffering, and human rights abuses in society and in the darker places of the world.

I believe the hearts of the fathers will turn to the children and the hearts of the children to the fathers.

I believe the generations will work together to accomplish incredible change on the earth.

I believe there will be intimacy with God with worship that never ends like it was in David's tabernacle.

I also believe there will be the wisdom and wealth of Solomon's reign.

I believe there will be an entirely new level of understanding of the written Word of God, and a greater ability to interpret the prophetic books of Daniel and Revelation.

I believe there will be clear prophetic words about immediate future events.

There will surely also be many wonderful phenomena that I have failed to describe. I do believe that these will all take place, and they will come together in a spectacular finale in such a powerful way that the gospel will surely be available to every man, woman and child on the face of the earth. In a matter of a few years, I believe a truly unprecedented multitude of souls will be harvested and brought into the Kingdom of God.

CRISES AND CHAOS

Politicians and revolutionaries know the importance of taking advantage of crises and chaos in a nation to bring quick change. One politician made the statement, "You don't want to waste a good crisis." God will allow a certain amount of crises to wake a nation up to their need. If people lose their jobs or fortunes, or if chaos occurs in the financial markets, people begin to realize that there is nothing they can put their trust in but God. When things go well, people don't feel their need for God, but when crisis occurs, they begin to call on God.

I believe that in addition to all the other preparations, God has allowed man's greed and selfishness to produce a harvest of financial suffering, in order to soften the hearts of the people. There are financial and political crises in America and throughout most of the world today. These will not end for some time, and more and more people will call on the name of the Lord for help. The timing of these crises will prepare the hearts of unbelievers to receive the help God's people will offer them in both the natural and spiritual.

ADDRESSING YOUR QUESTIONS

I realize that many readers will be quite skeptical or unbelieving of such unusual prophecies. Let me address some objections and questions:

1. What about opposition and persecution? I'm glad you asked that question. It certainly is important to be prepared for whatever the enemy throws at us. I do expect the church to face op-

position and persecution throughout the harvest period. I just believe that the enemy will have no weapons to compare with God's shock and awe demonstration, which will catch him off guard. I do believe that his opposition will increase, and as the harvest time comes to a close, those who have easily received Christ as Savior will have their faith and commitment tested. I personally believe the antichrist spirit will rise up after the harvest to separate the wheat from the chaff. You can't separate the wheat from the chaff until you have harvested the wheat. However, our purpose in this book is not to define our eschatology, but simply prophesy the coming ultimate convergence.

2. How will Christians handle so much wealth without becoming greedy and carnal? The fact is we are somewhat greedy and carnal without the wealth, but it does manifest more when wealth arrives. It's only when we are so in love with Jesus, as they were in the early church, that wealth, fame, power and control lose their appeal. There is nothing to compare with His manifest presence and the excitement it brings to our spirits. His presence also purifies our hearts and makes our consciences more sensitive to right and wrong. I believe that this level of intimate presence will continue long enough to bring in the world-wide harvest.
3. Where is the Scripture to prove these prophecies? As I mentioned at the beginning, there are no clear black and white Scriptures stating what I am predicting. There are few biblical prophecies of future events that are clear in black and white; they are cloaked in mystery and symbolism. I have read Revelation many times, as have many great scholars. Equally great minds have come up with totally different interpretations of that book.

There are a number of verses that can be seen to promote the view I have put forth, and several were mentioned in this book. We know that Jesus talked much about the harvest at the end of the age. Do we believe He will have a meager harvest or a great one? I believe it will be a great harvest worthy of the King of Kings. We have brought together many Scriptures and combined them with what many contemporary prophets are saying and then added what we believe God has revealed to us.

I have long been convinced of this simple prophetic scenario. God is preparing an army of lovers and worshippers who are willing and ready to go to the ends of the earth for Him, and they will lay down their lives or do whatever He asks of them. When the number of them reaches the number that God is looking for and they have been adequately prepared and trained, God will release the resources through the great transfer of wealth and empower them to go to the ends of the earth.

God told me to start a Sending Center to send out workers into the harvest fields. I hadn't ever heard of such a thing, but it was quickly confirmed through a very accurate prophet who spoke the same words that God had spoken to my heart. Before long, God reminded me of the Scripture – "How shall they preach unless they be sent?" (Romans 10:15) Many would go if they were sent. I believe that "sending" includes financing their journey. Probably millions of Christians in America, and many more millions in other countries of the world, would love to take the gospel to other people groups and nations, if only there was provision for them to go. I believe God will use us to provide the finances to train and send thousands of them without them having to beg friends and churches for support.

4. How long will it take to happen? That's another excellent question. From all the information I have on the subject, I believe it's a matter of years, not decades. I believe the harvest has begun and that the transfer of wealth is being prepared. I believe ideas are being downloaded from Heaven for new inventions that will be released in the perfect timing of God. A number of prophets have had visits to Heaven where they have seen some of the inventions and blueprints, etc., which will be released at the proper time to the right people. Perhaps you, the reader,

will be a recipient of one of these special assignments, so you can be used by God in some unique way to provide tools to others for the harvest. It's really a very important time to listen for the voice of God.

That's all the questions I'm hearing at the moment, so let's wrap this up. God will not forget His covenants with His people from the beginning of time. He will not forget His purpose for creating man. He will provide Himself a place to dwell in the midst of His people, and He will not be stingy providing resources for that place. It will be much more magnificent than Solomon's Temple, and it will be filled with people from every tribe and nation. He will receive at least a tithe of the world's population, but I believe it will be a double tithe, if not more.

So how do we get ready? Worship Him, worship Him and worship Him some more. Listen and obey everything He asks you to do, but always come back to worship Him and exalt His name above all others. Read the Scriptures and ask Him for understanding and wisdom to interpret it for the day in which you live. Stay humble and keep a servant's heart. Open your heart to the poor and oppressed. Get involved in changing your world for the better whenever you can, as long as you have the approval of your Guide, the Holy Spirit.

Keep your eyes on the skies for the coming of the Great and Ultimate Convergence out of Heaven. You may see the signs that signal that it's on the way to the place where you live. Get excited! There's never been a better time in which to live on this earth. We are a chosen generation, a royal priesthood, a holy nation, and we should be giving God continuous praise for allowing us to be His child, His friend, and His bride.

Most of all, praise Him for the privilege of bringing joy to His heart and fulfilling the purpose for which He created us. Give Him pleasure by sharing your heart with His and allowing Him to share His heart with you – like best friends would do. That's why He created you and that's the only thing that will bring fulfillment to your heart and to His.

SHALOM!!!

BEN R. PETERS

With over 40 years of ministry experience, Ben Peters with his wife, Brenda, have been called to an international apostolic ministry of equipping and activating others with a passion for sending laborers into the harvest fields of the earth, including the seven mountains of society. As founders and directors first of Open Heart Ministries, and now the Kingdom Sending Center, Ben and Brenda have ministered to tens of thousands with teaching and prophetic ministry. The result is that many have been saved, healed, delivered and activated into powerful ministries of their own.

Ben has been given significant insights for the body of Christ and has written sixteen books in the past ten years, since beginning a full-time itinerant ministry. His passions and insights include unity in the body of Christ, accessing the glory of God, five-fold team ministry, prophetic ministry, and signs and wonders for the world-wide harvest.

Kingdom Sending Center
P.O. Box 25
Genoa, IL 60135

www.KingdomSendingCenter.org
ben.peters@kingdomsendingcenter.org

Kings and Kingdoms
Anointing a New Generation of Kings
to Serve the King of Kings
by Ben R. Peters

Finding Your Place
on Your Kingdom Mountain
A Practical Guide and Workbook for Reigning
as Kings in the Kingdom of God
by Ben R. Peters

Designed for Study or Group Discussion

Veggie Village and the Great and Dangerous Jungle
An Allegory
by Ben R. Peters

Available from Kingdom Sending Center
www.kingdomsendingcenter.org

God Is So God!

The Adventures of a Traveling Ministry
on a Prophetic Faith Journey
by Brenda Peters

God's Favorite Number
The Secret Keys and Awesome
Power of True Unity
by Ben R. Peters

Resurrection!
A Manual for Raising the Dead
by Ben R. Peters

Signs and Wonders
To Seek or Not to Seek
by Ben R. Peters

With Me
A Captivating Journey Into Intimacy
by Ben R. Peters

Holy Passion: Desire on Fire
Igniting the Torch of Godly Passion
by Ben R. Peters

Catching Up
to the
Third World
Seven Indispensable Keys
To EXPLOSIVE Revival
In the Western Church
BEN R. PETERS

Birthing the Book Within You
Inspiration and Practical Help
to Produce Your Own Book
by Ben R. Peters

45665514R00080

Made in the USA
Charleston, SC
31 August 2015